THE Waters of Hermes
Le acque di Ermes

Studi & Testi 3

directed by

Luigi Monga & Dino S. Cervigni

A COLLECTION OF MONOGRAPHS OF
ANNALI D'ITALIANISTICA
THE UNIVERSITY OF NORTH CAROLINA AT CHAPEL HILL
CHAPEL HILL, NC 27599-3170

THE WATERS OF HERMES
LE ACQUE DI ERMES

Proceedings of a Festival
of Italian Poetry & Myth

The College of Charleston
Charleston, South Carolina
Lightsey Conference Center, March 18-20, 1999

Edited
by

MASSIMO A. MAGGIARI

Annali d'italianistica, Inc.
Chapel Hill, NC 27599-3170

AdI, Studi & Testi 3
A collection of monographs sponsored by
Annali d'italianistica, Inc.
and directed by Luigi Monga & Dino S. Cervigni.
The University of North Carolina at Chapel Hill
Chapel Hill, NC 27599-3170

Library of Congress Control Number: 00-131648

MASSIMO A. MAGGIARI
    THE WATERS OF HERMES/LE ACQUE DI ERMES
    1.   Poetry: Italian & English.
    2.   Criticism, theory, interpretation.
    3.   Italian literature; comparative literature.

    ISBN 0-9657956-2-4

This book is dedicated to
Alfred C. Olivetti

Contents

Festival Opening

THE WATERS OF HERMES
LE ACQUE DI ERMES

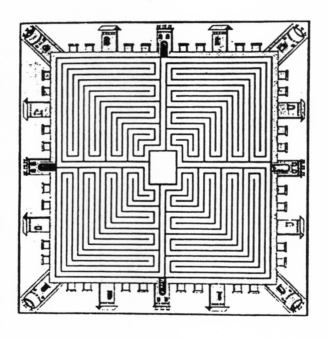

Massimo A. Maggiari

The Waters of Hermes:
A Festival of Poetry and Myth

The philosophers call me Mercury. My consort is philosophical gold. I am the old dragon you can find anywhere in the terrestrial globe. I descend to earth and ascend to the heavens. I am the highest and the lowest, I am the highest and the heaviest. . . . My waters and my fire destroy and then restore. . . .

(Carl Gustav Jung, Alchemical Studies CW 13)

One October afternoon in 1997, Giuseppe Conte and I, strolling in downtown Charleston, had the idea to organize a festival of poetry and myth at the College of Charleston. Every step we took, our enthusiasm grew with our intuition and we slowly arrived at an overall vision of the cultural event and all it would entail.

We would alternate readings of poetry and essays and include a series of invocations in classical Greek to ancient divinities. The absolute lord of this event would be Hermes, the Latin Mercury. In this figure we recognized a powerfully symbolic force and the catalytic role of poetic guide. Moreover, we would associate Hermes to that element that, owing to its fluidity and volatility, is closer to his changing nature: water. The event was intended to be a rite, magical invocation, dialoguing reflection, poetic word, testimonial, and philosophical discourse.

The three days of the festival would have facilitated the progressive bursting forth of the enchanting and regenerative spirit of the waters of Hermes: the arcane substance that in alchemical procedures is present as *mercurius crudus*. This divine, light, live water that paradoxically does not wet our hands cohabits with the soul of the world, to the extent that it entrusts the intellect to another way of feeling, another way of seeing, and another way of imagining.

We came to an agreement, and the event was set forth for March 1999, in Charleston, on the southern shores of the New World. Months of feverish preparations, calls, faxes, and e-mails followed, together with meetings and presentations in Italy. The guests would come to South Carolina from Georgia, New York, California, and North

The Waters of Hermes/Le acque di Ermes. Edited by Massimo A. Maggiari.

Carolina, from Europe and South Africa. An archipelago of atolls and arched bridges, slender and solitary old villas, and the moist facades of hanging gardens welcomed the participants after their exhausting trips.

While I write these brief introductory remarks, the days of the festival are etched in the history of Charleston and its College and in the memory of the participants and public. *The Waters of Hermes* has left a deep furrow, and a future edition of this event has been set two years from now.

With myth and poetry, Italian culture has landed on the southeastern shore of the United States. A new and adventurous way has been traced through the marshes and the magic horizon of South Carolina.

We wish that the mythopoetic yearning of the soul, in the hopes for a new spirituality and redemptive consciousness, will take over the new millennium. We wish that once again Hermes, wrapped in the darkness of his mantle, will appear unexpectedely and guide us among the live oaks, with hanging Spanish moss, of the Low Country.

The College of Charleston

***

We would like to thank the generous contribution of the Dino Olivetti Foundation, Gividi U.S.A., Lati U.S.A., and the Mediterranean Shipping Company. We would also like to express our gratitude to the National Italian American Foundation for its generous support of the publication of the Conference Proceedings.

We would like to thank the *Circolo Italiano*, the *Club Italiano*, Provost Conrad P. Festa, Dean Sam M. Hines, the Department of Foreign Languages, the Department of English, the Department of Philosophy and Religious Studies, the Department of Communication Sciences, and the Department of Classics of the College of Charleston.

We would like to acknowledge the key participation of Jorge Marbán and Flaminio Di Biagi in organizing the festival. Special thanks should also go to Tom Heeney and all the readers of the poems' English translations.

Finally, a special recognition goes to Laura Stortoni-Hager for translating the poems from Italian into English and for her continuous availability throughout every phase of the festival.

Conrad D. Festa

Welcoming Remarks

It is my privilege and my honor to welcome you all to the College of Charleston. I am especially pleased to have our guests, the artists, here among our students, our faculty, our staff and our community because they clearly bring to us the opportunity to widen our vision, extend the frontiers of our experience, and deepen our sensibilities. Although this festival honors Hermes and all that he represents for the creative spirit, we are also here to honor the artists and scholars who come to us from a culture that has traditionally nurtured the creative spirit that dwells in all of us. So to you writers and scholars among us today, I extend my heartiest welcome.

The subject of this Festival, symbol and myth, also fills me with pleasant anticipation. As a professor of literature, I introduce my students to the concept that symbol and myth are humanity's guides to truth that lies too deep for human tears: no mere intellectual discipline or exercise can get us there. Furthermore only imagination can provide us access to ineffable truths and transcendent knowledge. And those are the tools of the artist's trade.

Therefore, we come this week in anticipation of a very special joy. It is the same joy that bathes us during that wonderful moment when we experience sunlight filtering through scarlet and golden leaves or that washes over us in powerful waves when we hear the soaring harmonies of a brass ensemble in a lofty cathedral. It is that pure joy which brings us peace and a confirmation of deep truths we share with all those among us and all those who have ever come before us. We are ready, then, to cast our nets into the waters of symbol, myth, and the imagination.

I anticipate that the catch of the day will be tremendous.

Thank you all for being with us.

Giuseppe Conte and Massimo A. Maggiari

A Dialogue

What is *Mitomodernismo*?

I can only speak about my own idea, my personal view of *Mitomodernismo*. First of all, unlike at the beginning of the century, it is not an organized movement. Of all the poets invited to be here from Italy, only Tomaso Kemeny was deeply involved with the foundation of the movement. But also the others present today— poets whom I regard as the best of our generation in Italy—are in agreement that there is a relationship between myth and poetry, although everyone of us has a different style.

Mitomodernismo is a literary group that opens a new direction towards the place where myth and soul, soul and language, language and cosmos are connected. In this way, anyone of you (pointing at the public) can be *mitomodernista*!

What do I mean when I say the word *Mitomodernismo*? In my opinion, both in the fields of poetry and narrative, *Mitomodernismo* means all of the following: 1) to bring the metamorphic and primordial energy of myth into our language and our work; 2) to rediscover the living presence of ancient gods in nature and in our language, in our soul and in everyday life; 3) to overcome the typical idea of the crisis in Western civilization, to overcome materialism and nichilism; 4) to find the new springs of spirituality, connecting our culture with other civilizations, making spiritual energies meet, exploring the universe of different cultures, such as the native American culture, the Sufi and Hindu philosophies, and so on; 5) to connect poetry again with prophecy; 6) to reconnect poetry and the dream of the future; 7) to rediscover, through our literary work, the power of eroticism as manifested in soul, heroism, nature, cosmos and myth. Thus,

Mitomodernismo is something that we must reinvent and create in every moment.

How different is your way of dealing with myth in this new literary approach?

For *Mitomodernismo*, myth is not an archeological recreation. It is a form of knowledge. In our century, many writers, the most relevant in the literary field, have written just to demonstrate that the glorious myth of the gods is not dead, and that it is possible now to create new myths. *Mitomodernismo* challenges the thesis of the death of myth and of the impossibility of its re-creation. *Mitomodernismo* believes, just as the poets in the Romantic Age did—and before that, the Italian Renaissance poets—that the role of the poet is that of shaman, traveller, and warrior of the spirit. *Mitomodernismo* has its roots in the Romantic age, when poets dreamed of renewing the world and of creating new visions of the soul.

What is the role of Hermes in this new approach to literature and myth?

Hermes is a minor god in the Greek pantheon, but we find him also, under different names, in the Egyptian pantheon as Anubis and Thot, in the Hindu pantheon as Pushan, in the German pantheon as Odin, and in the Celtic pantheon as Lug. According to the *Homeric Hymns*, Hermes was a newborn baby when he killed a tortoise, stripped it of its carapace, and applying seven strings to it, began to play and sing praises to Zeus and Maia, his parents. Hermes is a trickster, the god of thieves and liars, the protector of markets; but first of all, he is a messenger, an intermediary between gods and men, a guide, a very special kind of guide for the souls going to the Underworld. Therefore, I think that poetry has a continuous relationship with Hermes, because poetry invites us to speak with the shadows and brings us closer to their land, allowing us to see what is otherwise invisible and to fly around the world of the shadows. Hermes is the God of quickness and lightness, the very same god Calvino wrote about in the American Lectures. Now, only Hermes, not Dyonisus, not Apollo, can help us bring perspective to light and darkness, and to recapture in our language the enchantment of everyday life.

POETRY

GIUSEPPE CONTE

Giuseppe Conte was born in Liguria in 1945. He has published five books o poetry. The last one, published in 1997, is *Canti d'Oriente e d'Occidente/Song of the East and the West*. He is also the author of six novels. The last one bear the title: *Il ragazzo che parla col sole/The boy who speaks to the sun*. He ha written on myth for many years and in 1999 has written *Il sonno degli Dei/Th sleep of the Gods* and *Il passaggio di Ermes/The passage of Hermes*.

Giuseppe Conte's poems are translated by Laura Stortoni-Hager.

The Last Drug-Addicted Boy

The last drug-addicted boy died
on the seashore, thrown away
like an apple core, eaten and
fragile, impotent against the continuity
of the undertow, encrusted with grains
of resplendent sand, a humble
organic remnant, blackened, already
decaying.
He was the last one, we no longer know
his first name or his last, nor
what he was looking for

From *L'oceano e il ragazzo*

L'ultimo ragazzo drogato

L'ultimo ragazzo drogato è morto in
riva al mare, gettato come un
torsolo di mela, mangiato e
fragile, impotente contro la continuità
della risacca, incrostato di grani
di sabbia splendente, lui umile
residuo organico, annerito, già
in via di corrompimento.
Era l'ultimo, di lui non si sa più
il nome né il cognome, né che cosa
cercava

***

One day if the reader of the third millennium
will read me, he will know that there were trees
and desires, palms and pines, and eucalyptus
with leaves shaped like crescent moons,

and roses: there were those who no longer
wanted to suffer, those who wanted to love everything,
and those who made a gift of themselves and of poems
that were violent and distant, simple and

weak

From *L'oceano e il ragazzo*

***

Un giorno se mi leggerà il lettore del
terzo millennio, saprà che c'erano gli
alberi e i desideri, le palme e i pini, e gli
eucalipti dalle foglie a quarto di luna, e le
rose: chi non voleva più soffrire, e chi
voleva amare tutto, chi di se
stesso faceva dono e dei poemi
violenti e lontani erano, semplici e

deboli

***

Archeologist of my days, I exhume
the names of the trees, and flowers, through whose
fields of destruction no white man has ever
wept: we no longer remember anything,

not the acrid smell of the roots, nor the immense
swelling of tides, nor the months that the moon
announces with red grass or with the pale reddening
branches: dreams and desires, they too are

buried

From *L'oceano e il ragazzo*

***

Archeologo dei miei giorni, dissotterro
i nomi degli alberi, dei fiori, per i cui
campi di sterminio nessun bianco ha mai
pianto: non ricordiamo più nulla, né

l'odore acre delle radici, né l'alzarsi
immenso delle maree né i mesi che la
luna annuncia con l'erba rossa o con il
rosa sui rami: i sogni e i desideri anch'essi

sepolti

***

Do not drive your camels so fast,
young camel driver, long is the track

in the desert. Don't you see how thirsty they are,
how hungry they are,

how they yearn for the grass of their native soil?
The deserts have left only skin to their bodies

to cover the bones that protrude.
They fear the summits of the dunes, the turbid

winds that unleash themselves up there,
the cold stars whirling in the night.

Yet they proceed exhausted
on the sand that yields and burns.

Do not spur them. Let them go
at their own pace where they want to go:

time passes too quickly already.
And even your heart feels it.

From *Canti d'Oriente e d'Occidente*

***

Non guidare così in fretta i tuoi cammelli
giovane cammelliere, lunga è la pista

nel deserto. Non vedi come hanno sete,
non vedi come hanno fame, come bramano

l'erba della loro terra natale?
I deserti hanno lasciato solo la pelle

ai loro corpi, a ricoprire ossa sporgenti,
temono le cime delle dune, i venti

torbidi che vi si scatenano,
le stelle fredde a vortice nella notte.

Eppure estenuati procedono
sulla sabbia che cede e brucia.

Non incitarli, lascia che vadano
col loro passo dove sanno andare:

fa già presto il tempo a passare.
E questo sente anche il tuo cuore.

***

I am here, sitting on a carpet
of leaves and spring blossoms,

and my silence is a prayer.
With me I have wine and a goblet.

If only my Beloved were near me,
if her shining mouth were here!

The scent of her kisses
is sweeter than jasmine.

They say I am wise
because I know all of God's words

and I know that his face is invisible
though He bestows purple and fire

on all the rose bushes.
But I am wise because I drink, I gamble,

I sing while time ravages us.
How many roses will open this morning

and how many more will fall tomorrow
or wither under the gusts

of the hurricanes! Time makes us brothers —
we who move under the same sky.

Isn't it the same for us all —
that moon that looks like a pomegranate

slowly detaching from its branch?
But I am wise because I love.

From *Canti d'Oriente e d'Occidente*

***

Sono qui seduto su un tappeto
di foglie e fiori di primavera,

e il mio silenzio è una preghiera
ed ho con me la coppa e il vino.

Se la mia Amata fosse vicino
se la sua bocca lucente fosse qui.

Il profumo dei suoi baci
è più dolce del gelsomino.

Dicono che sono saggio perché
conosco tutte le parole di Dio

e so che il suo volto non si vede
ma a tutti i roseti concede

la sua porpora e il suo fuoco.
Ma io sono saggio perché bevo, gioco,

canto mentre il tempo ci rapina.
Quante rose si apriranno stamattina

e quante ne cadranno domani
o sotto le raffiche degli uragani

avvizziranno. Il tempo ci affratella
noi che ci muoviamo sotto lo stesso cielo.

Non è la stessa per noi tutti quella
luna che sembra una melagrana

staccata lentamente dal suo ramo?
Ma io sono saggio perché amo.

***

There is a sweetness deep down in life
that I would not exchange for anything

that belongs to heaven.
It's when, for mysterious reasons,

begin the tepid miracles of a dawn

of kisses

between two mouths until then
foreign.

From *Canti d'Oriente e d'Occidente*

***

Cè una dolcezza giù nella vita
che non cambierei con niente

di ciò che appartiene al cielo.
E' quando chissà da che, perché cominciano

tra due bocche estranee sino ad allora
i miracoli tiepidi d'aurora

dei baci.

Let's Do Business Again

Democracy, I hated you in the irises of the boys abandoned
in the quick of their dreams,
for your demand that numbers be the factor deciding destiny
for your adoring at the Temple only merchandise and paper money
I hated you when you trampled on poetry, your secret mother
when you extinguished the leaf-wave song of the universe
when you disarmed the strong, when you left the spirit to die
I hated you for spreading cowardly envy, profiteering, and lies.

But you, true democracy — flowering —
You new democracy that we can still engender,
the democracy that Whitman wanted, great with trees, lakes, desires,
bodies, communal journeys and songs, companions, joys,
democracy, new race

Today I, Giuseppe, born in 1945
at the age of forty-five years, having passed the threshold
neither blind nor prophet
against those who kill the gods with an edict
against those who govern with tanks and swords
against those who have no pity for the fallen
against those who exile, exterminate, imprison
against immobility, uniformity and order
against the voice of spies turned masters

I choose you

It is not true that freedom can do without leaves and waves, that you can
do without heroes

Democracy, let's do business again

From *Dialogo del poeta e del messaggero*

Ristabiliamo commercio

Democrazia, ti ho odiata nelle iridi dei ragazzi abbandonate dal vivo dei sogi
nella tua pretesa che sia il numero a decidere il destino
nel tuo adorare al Tempio soltanto la mercanzia e la carta moneta
ti ho odiata quando hai calpestato la poesia tua madre segreta
quando hai spento il canto foglie—onde dell'universo
quando hai disarmato i forti, hai lasciato lo spirito morire
ti ho odiata per il tuo diffondere l'invidia imbelle, il profittare, il mentire.

Ma tu democrazia vera, fioriture
tu democrazia nuova, che ancora possiamo generare
che Whitman voleva, grande d'alberi, laghi, desideri,
corpi, viaggi insieme e canti, compagni, gioie,
democrazia nuova stirpe

oggi io Giuseppe nato nel 1945
a quarantacinque anni, varcato il limite
né cieco né profeta
contro chi uccide con un editto gli dei
contro chi governa attraverso i carri e le spade
contro chi non ha pietà per chi cade
contro chi esilia, stermina, imprigiona
contro l'immobilità, l'uniformità, l'ordine
la voce delle spie fatta padrona

io ti scelgo.

Non è vero che la libertà può fare a meno di foglie e
di onde, e tu di eroi.

Democrazia, ristabiliamo commercio tra noi.

The First Messenger

He was waiting in front of my house, on the threshold.
Tall, bent over, eyes half—closed, without wings.
I was seeing him for the first time,

but I knew that he was there for me.
Bent over as if he carried a tree-trunk
on his skinny shoulders,

as if he came from too far away—
his body made of a substance
more akin to ash than flesh.

His eyes half-closed, as if
within a young white rose, shirt
unbuttoned around his neck, jacket

dusty, but not from pebbles or pine needles,
his white hair thinning: "Giuseppe,
You have come back," he said. It was just

noon, on a spring day.
The sky was bright, as if it were screaming.
I put down my suitcase where the ivy cascaded,

foamy, at the foot of the wall,
beyond the oleanders and the plum tree.
He spoke with a soft voice, the messenger.

From *Dialogo del poeta e del messaggero*

Il primo messaggero

Mi aspettava davanti a casa mia, sulla porta.

Alto, curvo, senz'ali, gli occhi socchiusi:
io lo vedevo per la prima volta,

ma lo pensai, che era lì per me.
Curvo come se avesse portato
sulle sue spalle smagrite un tronco

d'albero, come se venisse da troppo
lontano, il corpo di una sostanza
più simile alla cenere che alla carne.

Gli occhi socchiusi, quasi dentro una giovane
rosa bianca: una camicia sbottonata
al collo, una giacca impolverata

né dalla ghiaia né dagli aghi di pino,
i capelli radi e schiariti: "Giuseppe,
sei tornato" mi disse. Era appena

passato mezzogiorno, di primavera.
Il cielo urlava tanto aveva luce.
Posai la borsa dove cadeva l'edera

spumosa, ai piedi del muro,
di là degli oleandri e del susino.
Parlava a voce bassa, il messaggero.

All the Wonder of the World

It's as you say, I should leave again
I've never been happy in a house.
I've never been happy in a family.
I've never felt homesick when I was
alone and far away. All the wonder
of the world was on the promenade
by the sea, when, school books in my satchel,
I walked fast and breathed in
wind the color of salt and agave.
I pretended to have my hand
in a girl's hand: the wonder, the strong race
of dreams, the books, the movies,
the long train rides,
the long crossing of the soul ...
But the walls of a house, never.

From *Dialogo del poeta e del messaggero*

Tutta la meraviglia del mondo

È come dici tu, dovrei ripartire.
Non sono mai stato felice in una casa.
Non sono mai stato felice in famiglia.
Non ho mai avuto nostalgia, quando ero
solo e lontano. Tutta la meraviglia
del mondo per me era la passeggiata
alta sul mare quando, i libri di scuola
in una cartella, a passo veloce
andavo, e inspiravo il vento
colore del salino e delle agavi
e fingevo di avere una ragazza
per mano: la meraviglia, la razza
forte dei sogni, i libri, il cinema,
i lunghi viaggi in treno,
le lunghe traversate dell'anima
ma mai i muri di una casa, mai.

GABRIELLA GALZIO

Gabriella Galzio was born in Rome in 1956 and presently works as a translator in Milan. She has translated several German authors and has published two books of poetry. The last one, in 1996, is entitled *La buia preghiera/The Dark Prayer*. Gabriella Galzio is the founder and co-editor of the literary journal *Fare Anima/Soul-making*.

Gabriella Galzio's poems are translated by Laura Stortoni-Hager.

With you I fascinated the roses,
the long foolishness, the ecstatic raptures—
dare—the anxiety that translates,
that turns into an object, sending out
limpid calls from the marshes:
with you I blunted the ax on the
weave

that talks of itself, that smoothes itself
that becomes elongated, but to you
I did not give a rose, for you I did not
tremble in my armor, I did not
steal, betray, lose, lie.
You have not been a lighthouse, nor
the seat of a debacle around it
I have only attached—the rocks on the peer
and the long regret of the thunder—
to a snapshot, to a plaster bust

From *La buia preghiera*

Con te ho fascinato le rose
le lunghe idiozie, i rapimenti
estatici, osa, l'ansia che si traduce
che si fa cosa, e manda
di palude limpidi richiami
:con te ho rovinato l'ascia
sulla trama

che narra di sé, che s'appiana
s'allunga, ma a te
non ho dato rosa, non ho
tremato nella corazza, non ho
rubato, tradito, perso, mentito
tu non sei stato, faro o
luogo di débâcle intorno ad esso
ho solo attinto—la scogliera del molo
e il rammarico lungo del tuono—
a una foto, a un busto di gesso

Choral Mother

"I will be for you a choral mother, I will hurl myself into the fire
I will not waver, nor infringe
I will be the free wrestling match, I will be the burning
field, the whip of the wheat in your golden temples.
I will be a limpid, urgent thought,
a drum beating on the plain
I will be women coming down in the open field
women who advance, who rise frontally
I will be war for war, a sudden movement in combat
the depth of the back scenes, a natural theater"

Madre corale

"Sarò per te madre corale, correrò nel fuoco
non avrò tentennamenti, infingimenti
sarò la lotta libera, il campo incendiato
la frusta del grano nell'oro delle tempie
sarò un pensiero limpido, urgente
un tamburo battente sulla piana
sarò donne che scendono in scenario aperto
donne che avanzano sorgono frontali
sarò guerra per guerra scatto in combattimento
profondità di quinte, teatro naturale."

Between the Forest and the Court

We will return, and, like us,
life in its splendor, the trees yellowing
the trunks undone by the dragging of the waters
blue, violet, a little harbor, the sun ...
We will have children, maybe, and a patch of land
A new poverty will invade the world
the courts will be emptied, the heretics will be freed
Blessed is he who does not intern himself in a labyrinth
Let me be blessed for hanging on to my bone,
a flowery life, here in the airy rooms
of thin stones, a soft language
adjusts a sylvan world
to your courtier-like palate.

But I remain, like Merlin the sorcerer,
between the forest and the court
in the thin place of this crossing
in the shadowy threshold of the wood
at the edge, an art of fire
within formulae. It is better to hide—
you can hide inside poetry—
than to come out in the open,
to tell the world in a drink,
and to dream the flight
that you cannot accomplish,
coming back into yourself
like a madman from a fit.
A desire for truth furrows the air,
a desire for truth
and an unaltered faith, white and hoisted,
has the brightness of a season of sparrows.

Fra la selva e la corte

Ce ne torneremo, come noi, la vita
nel suo fulgore, gli alberi ingialliti
i tronchi sfatti nel trascinarsi delle acque
blu, viola, un porticciolo, il sole
avremo figli, forse, e un angolo di orto
una nuova povertà invaderà il mondo
vuoteranno le corti, affrancheranno gli eretici
beato chi non si interna nel labirinto
beata me stretta a un osso di me
una vita fiorita, qui nelle stanze ventilate
di rade pietre, un esile linguaggio
aggiusta una parola di selva
per il tuo palato cortigiano.

Ma io, come Merlino, il mago
sto, fra la selva e la corte
nel luogo sottile del trapasso
nella soglia ombratile del bosco
al limitare, un'arte di fuoco
dentro formule. Meglio celarsi
—dietro la poesia ti puoi nascondere—
che venire allo scoperto, dire il mondo
in un sorso, berlo
e il volo che stenti a compiere
sognarlo, rientrando in te
come da furia un folle
solca nell'aria un desiderio di verità
e inalterata fede salda, bianca e inalberata
stagione dei passeri, ha il candore.

Sophia Generating the World

I beamed you on top of the cathedrals
I recognized you, you know, by those shadows,
the blue eye shadows, and the blind eyelids
You crossed the night, lightly, among stones,
white stones that took shape
We prayed a little, humbly, at the bottom
hungry, with the hunger of love
we were equal
in our bones, thin, knocked down by vertigo
To look at each other was the only fulfillment
It was there that I conceived you
more out of love than out of logic
We were reduced to the bare bones, to the frost
Yet you laughed, and your hands rhythmically
alternated flights and caresses; you were ensconced
within a smile, can one love not knowing?
Can one disconnect the meaning of things?
There is no other force sustaining the verse
that lays foundations on your steps
filling hardened tears with water
I was Sophia generating the world
and believing in it
                    was my first work.

Sofia che genera il mondo

Ti ho folgorato in cima a cattedrali
riconosciuto, sai, da quelle ombre
le occhiaie azzurre e le palpebre cieche
attraversavi la notte, leggero, fra pietre
bianchissime, prendevano forma
si pregava poco, umilmente
in fondo, nella fame
nella fame d'amore, eravamo uguali
in ossa, smagriti, atterrati da vertigini
guardarsi era il solo avverarsi
è stato lì che ti ho concepito
più per amore che per logica
eravamo ridotti all'osso, al gelo
eppure ridevi, ritmicamente le mani
alternavano voli e carezze, eri interno
a un sorriso, si può amare sconoscendo?
Si può sconnettere, il senso delle cose?
Non c'è altra forza che sostenga il verso
che poggiare fondamenta sui tuoi passi
colmando d'acqua lacrime indurite
ero Sofia che genera il mondo e
averci creduto
            è stata l'opera prima.

Exemplary Soul

I have played on fear the desire for you,
the agony father of darkness,
I have known the silence of the tear
—but the tear was mine, deeply mine—
that you wanted to extract from me,
to dig out of my heart a vein of sorrow—
but in that vein shining with water
an azure, cosmic, watered pannier drank

                                  a fire

generated itself, without father, without mother,
the lymph of the exemplary soul
the vegetal transparency, the rain water
and in the leaf, pure, a violet

                                  budded

And then, incredulous, we crossed woods.
Through what instances, passes and thoughts,
in the long darkness of winter,
did you not sow salt on the blade of a gutter!
Crumbs to the sparrows, on a thin ridge
and weak hawks—

Anima esemplare

Ho giocato sulla paura il desiderio di te
l'agonia padre della tenebra
ho conosciuto il silenzio della lacrima
ma era mia, profondamente mia la lacrima
che tu volevi estrarmi, estirparmi
dal cuore una vena di dolore
ma in quella vena luminosa d'acqua beveva
azzurrata cosmica acquata gerla
                                                    un fuoco
si generava da sé, senza padre né madre
la linfa dell'anima esemplare
trasparenza vegetale, acqua piovana
nella foglia germinava pura
                                                    una viola
Poi, increduli, varcammo boschi.
Per quali istanze, valichi, pensieri
nella lunga ombra invernale
seminasti sale su una lamina di gronda!
    — briciole ai passeri, su un esile crinale
e gracili sparvieri —

***

You did not begrudge your word
that budded, measured, ruffled,
as if it knew how to arm space with void, a red hot blade
to fill the body, to empty the mind.
We did not part
for such a little harbor, we ignored
the small details. We built temples,
we opened doors. One by one—other measures —
advancing. We moved
the threshold, foiling the attempts
of the predators who gorge on the wheat,
who imprison
god.

We filled our pockets with bread, with oil,
with poor things, your water flasks,
the few
roses.

We scattered the seed:
we were not stingy.

From *La buia preghiera*

***

Non lesinasti, la tua parola
che germinò, misurata, scomposta
come sapesse amare, di spazio
il vuoto, una lama infuocata
riempire il corpo, svuotare
la mente. Non ci lasciammo
per così poco porto, non ci perdemmo
su piccole misure. Costruimmo templi
ricavammo porte. Ad una ad una—ben altre
misure—avanzando. Spostammo
la soglia. Rendendo vano
il tentativo di predatori
che ingozzano il grano, che imprigionano
dio.

Riempimmo tasche, di pani, di olio
di povere cose. Le tue borracce
le poche
rose.

Spargemmo il seme:
non fummo gelosi.

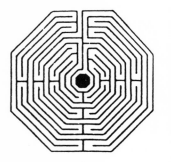

ROBERTO MUSSAPI

Roberto Mussapi was born in Cuneo in 1952 and presently works for the publishing house Jaca Books in Milan. He has published five books of poetry. The last one is entitled *La polvere e il fuoco/Dust and Fire* in 1997. He is also a playwright and has published four plays. In addition, he has translated poems by Lord Byron, Shelley, Keats, Melville and Stevenson.

Roberto Mussapi's poems are translated by Laura Stortoni-Hager, except *Enea's vision*, which is translated by Massimo A. Maggiari.

The Compassionate Goddess

To Giuseppe Conte

She came or maybe it was the curtain that told me
she had passed, but I
was looking for the only word to stop her.
It was too late to see her, yet not too late to wait
for her, for her who loved the loneliest man
on the enamel sea — and was not recognized.

Athena, they said, you who love him, welcome him
forever in your quiet, quell the waves
that wound his sides his memory.

She was foam, and he did not see her.
He floated in his raft, in his tatters.
There was a draft.
My room was empty,
the light circle of the lamp cold,
stainless steel.

For you, said the voice, but the lamp was turned off
in my mind earlier than in the room —
darkness came out of veins not mine
and my voice was no longer my voice.

Then, in the hour, recognized, spring returned.
It was still cold, every one was far away
in their raincoats, the wind made them look distant,
moved their volatile parts, the tissues.

La dea pietosa

a Giuseppe Conte

Venne o forse furono le tende a dirmi
che era passata, ma io
cercavo la sola parola per fermarla,
era tardi per vederla, non per attenderla
ancora, lei che amò l'uomo più solo
sul mare di smalto e non fu riconosciuta.

Atena, dissero, tu che l'ami, accoglilo
per sempre nella tua quiete, placa
le onde che gli feriscono i fianchi, la memoria.

Era schiuma e lui non la vide,
proseguiva nella sua zattera e nei suoi stracci,
era una corrente d'aria,
la mia stanza era vuota
il cerchio della lampada freddo,
inossidabile.

Per voi, disse la voce, ma la luce si era spenta
prima nella mia mente che nella stanza
e il buio uscì da vene non mie
non era mia la mia voce.

Poi, nell'ora, riconosciuta, tornò
la primavera e faceva ancora freddo
e tutti erano lontani negli impermeabili
il vento li distanziava, muoveva
la loro parte volatile, il tessuto.

The only one at the rudder who never spoke
during the voyage — they met him later,
she said. She was the one crying,
among the great foams, she cried human tears,
she melted.
You, brothers, you remain standing,
casting a shining shadow.
No one sits on this straw-thatched chair,
and the shadows have returned in the closet.
Grief and enchantment clot together,
they were bark.

It was she, Giuseppe, who passed through your life
like marine mist.
We saw her in the evening, almost faded, distant,
and with her were the echo and the returning words.
It did her no good to love you, to follow you
when you were a child up the slate steps in Porto Maurizio,
begging your father for mercy for you, for your street.

Today she descended in the shape of a girl
known to you, but I saw her
bend over your hands and cry,
then disappear towards Oneglia, leaving you
alone in front of the light of your shadow,
looming tall, perennial, by a sea of memory.

From *Gita Meridiana*

Uno solo al timone che non parlò
mai nel viaggio, poi lo incontrarono
disse, era lei che piangeva, tra le grandi schiume,
piangeva lei le lacrime umane,
si è sciolta.
Voi restate, fratelli, in piedi,
fate un'ombra lucente.

Nessuno siede su quella sedia di paglia
e le ombre sono tornate nel ripostiglio.
Dolore e incantesimo si raggrumano,
furono scorza.

Era lei, Giuseppe, che è passata nella tua vita
come una nebbia marina.
La vedemmo alla sera, quasi svanita, lontana.
E con lei l'eco e il ritorno delle parole,
a lei non è servito amarti, seguirti
su per le scale di Porto Maurizio da bambino, implorare
pietà al padre per te, per la tua strada.

Oggi è discesa in forma di ragazza
a te sconosciuta, ma io l'ho vista
chinarsi sulle tue mani e piangere
e scomparire verso Oneglia, lasciandoti
solo di fronte alla luce della tua ombra
e al mare della memoria perenne altissima.

Aeneas' Vision

Then there was the darkness of the branches,
so distant from the darkness of night, shady, blurred,
breathing with souls, and the waiting for her voice,
and a vegetal shiver in the black: and in front of us
the cave, the empty and desolate mouth of the Sibyl,
prophecy, air moved by the sound, pure voice.
And then the golden bough, and the promise
and the painful descent, and my father's shadow:
for you I submitted to the voice and darkness of the branches,
to see you again in the features drawn by time,
of your life and of my imprinted memory.
For you I accept the words coming out of rock,
and the blood that will be shed,
and the present dead and the future dead,
and our memory built on the dead.
And your image of shadow was called exile,
and I saw again Hector and his enemy crying for Patroclus,
Euryalus and Clorinda, and Lancelot's piety
and the blue partisans and all those
who fell to remember your shadow.
Many of them I recognized among enemy ranks.
In the morning I went out to fight them.

From *La polvere e il fuoco*

La visione di Enea

Poi fu il buio delle fronde
così lontano dal buio della notte, ombroso, mosso,
respirante di anime, e l'attesa della sua voce
e un brivido vegetale nel nero: e davanti a noi
l'antro, la bocca vuota e desolata della sibilla,
vaticinio, aria smossa dal suono, pura voce.
E poi il ramo d'oro, e la promessa,
e la dolorosa discesa, e l'ombra di mio padre:
per te mi sono piegato alla voce e al buio delle fronde,
per rivederti nei tratti disegnati dal tempo
della tua vita e della mia impressa memoria,
per te accetto le parole uscite dalla roccia,
e il sangue che sarà sparso,
e i morti presenti e i morti futuri,
e il nostro ricordo edificato sui morti.
E la tua immagine d'ombra si chiamava esilio,
e rividi Ettore e il suo nemico piangente per Patroclo,
Eurialo e Clorinda, e la pietà di Lancillotto
e i partigiani azzurri e tutti quelli
che caddero per ricordare la tua ombra.
Molti ne riconobbi nelle fila nemiche,
uscii nel mattino, per combatterli.

"Till When?"

"Till the time when the fabric will fall apart
and its fibers will become unattainable,
down to the last glance, the last memory."

"In the same cruelty of this October,
in the shudder of a rivulet, in this fall,
I feel almost the universal compassion
that precedes genesis, justifying it.
 "Why should it not survive us?"

"What remains of the explored land,
of the fields on which we have built our history,
if not a man,
one who drinks and bleeds,
the one to whom we pass on the legacy?"

From *La polvere e il fuoco*

"Fino a quando?"

"Fino a quando si sgretolerà il tessuto
e le fibre diventeranno inattingibili
anche all'ultimo sguardo, al ricordo."

"In questa stessa crudeltà di ottobre,
nel brivido del ruscello, in questa caduta
io sento come una compassione universale
che ha preceduto la genesi e la giustifica.
Perché non dovrebbe sopravviverci?"

"Che cosa resta della terra esplorata,
e dei campi su cui abbiamo edificato la nostra storia,
se non sarà un uomo,
uno che beve e sanguina,
quello a cui passeremo la staffetta?"

Word of Socrates for Birth and Death

I will miss this temple,
the marble light, the fresh shade of the columns
where my shadow annulled itself for an instant.
I will miss the work, the bench polished
till it reflects the light unknown by earth.
There is another work, now distant,
at the time of the hemlock and the coming death.
It does not belong to us; it is not mine, not yours,
it touches our life like a white ghost.
I have been her servant, even if I obeyed
the temple builders who work with marble,
even if I lived like a shadow waiting
to be able to love you differently, like a man
outside the semblance of a man, joined forever
to those who cried, in despair in the shadow of the temple.
The geometry of the stars is distant and present.
Yet I felt it, inside, I spoke for it —
though I was only a poor man, a servant
of the word and of change. Let me fly away as a lost soul,
white in the sky that whitens and fades,
leave me my freedom and my death.
Do not cry. Cry for the person I used to be
when I was near you, cry for yourselves,
the cold consolation of the stone, the tribute
to the city, the torment of cohabitation.
Let me die and lose myself in my return.

From *La polvere e il fuoco*

Parole di Socrate per nascita e morte

Avrò nostalgia di questo tempio,
la luce del marmo, l'ombra delle colonne
dove la mia ombra si annullava per un istante.
Nostalgia dell'opera, del bianco levigato
fino alla luce negata alla terra.
C'è un'altra opera, lontana, ora,
nel tempo della cicuta e della prossima morte.
Non ci appartiene, non è mia, vostra,
sfiora la nostra vita come un'ombra bianca.
Io sono stato suo servo, anche se ho obbedito
ai costruttori di templi che lavorano il marmo,
anche se ho vissuto come un'ombra in attesa
di potervi amare diversamente, uomo
fuori dalle spoglie dell'uomo e unito per sempre
a quelli che piansero disperati all'ombra del tempio.
La geometria delle stelle è lontana e presente,
io la sentivo, dentro, parlava per lei,
eppure ero solo un povero, un servo
della parola e del mutamento.
Lasciatemi volare via come perduto,
bianco nel cielo che sbianca e si perde,
lasciatemi la mia libertà e la mia morte.
Non piangete. Piangete
quello che fui accanto a voi, piangete voi stessi,
la fredda consolazione della pietra, il tributo
alla città, lo strazio della convivenza.
Lasciatemi morire e perdermi nel mio ritorno.

Letter from the Stone Age

This is a stone that I have chipped.
It was a long work in the night with little fire,
I finished it, I completed the work, so that I could
affix it to a dart and make it hit an object,
its death for my life.
I only wanted everything to shine,
and the circle of life and death
to enclose also my life within memory.
I did it for you, to survive,
even when I will be nothing more than a shadow
and you its repressed light:
you and I will be enclosed in the planet's circle
that time divides and that love confuses.

From *La polvere e il fuoco*

Lettera dall'età della pietra

Questa è una pietra da cui ho tolto le scaglie,
fu un lungo lavoro nella notte, poco fuoco,
la ultimai, conclusi l'opera,
perché affissa a una freccia colpisse l'oggetto,
la sua morte per la mia vita.
E io volevo solo che tutto splendesse,
che il cerchio della vita e della morte
chiudesse anche la mia vita nel ricordo.
L'ho fatto per te, per sopravvivere,
quando io non sarò più che un'ombra
e tu la sua luce repressa,
tu ed io chiusi nel cerchio del pianeta,
che il tempo divide e l'amore confonde.

Bewitched by a Star

It was a long journey, dune after dune, for the scribes.
For me, it was brief, so brief compared
to the motionless map of the stars.
I knew our destiny was the track:
to get out of it or to lose oneself in the sands.
Slow was the glance of the stars I knew,
studying their position and light.
The signs of the sky, the eternal routes,
as we glided like waves towards a death
were as soft as the caress of a woman at sunset.
I knew the celestial perfection and the brief
human breath extinguished after love-making.
Life — to vanish before the horizon.
I have known the cosmos and the Chaldean theories,
the stones still burning with the memory of Venus,
the designs of heaven jealously guarded in carpets' weave.
Then it was cave and darkness and animal
breath and poor limbs, and a distant obscurity
closer to earth, more distant than the stars.
I did not look inside. I felt compassion
for the smell, the poor heat of the gathered bodies.
I looked at a man passing near me,
his eyes staring, enraptured by a star.
Brown, dirty, with the tight shoulders of an idiot,
he drank light as if it were eternal.
I will remember him forever, I will tell his story.
Because it was not a reflection, rather a clash
between that night known to me and another obscure one
that chained him firmly to the sky.

L'incantato della stella

Fu un lungo viaggio, duna su duna, per gli scribi.
Per me fu breve, breve in confronto
all'immobile mappa delle stelle.
Sapevo che il nostro destino era la pista,
o uscirne, perdersi nelle sabbie,
lentezza era lo sguardo degli astri,
che ho conosciuto, studiandone posizione e luce.
I segni del cielo, le rotte eterne,
e noi scivolanti come onde verso una morte lieve
come la carezza di una donna al tramonto.
Conoscevo la perfezione celeste e il breve respiro
umano che si estingue dopo un atto d'amore.
La vita, svanire prima dell'orizzonte.
Ho conosciuto il cosmo e le teorie caldaiche,
le pietre che sfiammano del ricordo di Venere,
i disegni del cielo gelosamente custoditi nei tappeti.
Poi la grotta e fu buio e respiro
animale e povere membra, e una lontana
oscurità rasoterra, più lontana delle stelle,
io non guardai dentro, io provai pena
del tanfo, del povero calore di corpi raccolti.
E uno ne guardai che mi passava accanto,
con gli occhi fissi rapiti da una stella.
Bruno, sporco, con le spalle chiuse da idiota
beveva la luce come eternamente,
eternamente io lo ricorderò, lo racconto.
Perché non fu riflesso ma scontro,
tra quella luce a me nota e un'altra oscura
che in modo assoluto lo incatenava al cielo.

What light, what source, what stupefying stone
directed his glance, his body, and his destiny in the world? Because I
was already inside him and I watched him,
as I had watched the celestial enigmas,
and I do not know the light of the depths,
nor the breath of the ventricular cavern and the darkness,
and the map drawn and lost of his unknown existence.
What way, what track, what dunes raised by the wind
lead to that secret within yourself?
Where was the light, up in the sky or down low?
And how will I not get lost
as I explore a new universe,
when I follow you in the dark of your internal world?
On what points will I orient my voyage,
seeking the obscure route that your glance projected,
you, piece of earth, muddy, akin to me, brother?

Che luce, che fonte, che pietra stupefacente
orientò lo sguardo e il corpo e il suo destino nel mondo?
Perché io ero già in lui e lo scrutavo
come avevo scrutato gli enigmi celesti,
e non conoscevo la luce del profondo,
il fiato della caverna ventricolare e del buio
e la mappa disegnata e persa nella sua ignota esistenza.
Che strada, che pista, che dune alzate dal vento
portano a quel segreto entro te stesso?
Dov'era la luce, in alto o in basso?
E io come farò a non perdermi
per esplorare un nuovo universo
quando ti seguirò nel buio del tuo mondo interno,
su quali punti orienterò il mio viaggio
cercando la rotta oscura che proiettò il tuo sguardo,
tu, pezzo di terra,
fangoso simile, fratello?

The Night of August 10th

Do not cry, Haroun, on this August night
when the stars fall and their light dissolves
in the dark like sand when we sleep:
if they were always fixed and immutable they would be foreign to you,
and their motionless splendor would offend your flesh.
Imagine they descend out of celestial compassion,
an incarnation of stars that turn to dust,
molecules of light penetrating one another in the dark.
Remember the story of the bedouin Habib who fell in love with a firefly
and lived every instant of light watching her,
desperate when he saw her die one night.
But after years of weeping in the frost of the desert,
suddenly one night he saw her again
shining high in a fixed star:
the firefly, the wandering one, the phenomenal light,
returning from the sky to the illiterate bedouin.
Neither you, sultan, nor the poor bedouin,
have cried for a star or for a firefly,
but for the only thing for which a man cries:
a woman. There was the grief of lost light,
an astral premonition of a time fading away,
the extinction already included in the wound of the miracle,
and the distance from the sky, death.
Learn from the bedouin, love her as one loves a firefly,
give yourself at every moment of survival.
And when she appears to have been lost in the night
you will suddenly discover in her eyes
the high light of the fixed stars,
and in her, who seemed to dissolve in an August night,
you will find mortal affinity with you who beg her.

From *La polvere e il fuoco*

La notte del dieci agosto

Non piangere, Harun, in questa notte d'agosto
quando le stelle cadono e la loro luce si dissolve
nel buio come la sabbia nel sonno:
se fossero sempre fisse e immutabili ti sarebbero estranee,
e il loro splendore immobile offenderebbe la tua carne.
Immagina che scendano per una compassione celeste,
incarnazione d'astri che si disfanno in polvere,
molecole di luce che si compenetrano al buio,
ricorda la storia del beduino Habib che si innamorò di una lucciola
e visse ogni istante della sua luce guardandola,
e disperò vedendola morire in una notte.
Ma dopo anni di pianto nel gelo del deserto
una notte all'improvviso lui la rivide
risplendere alta in una stella fissa:
la lucciola, l'errante, la luce fenomenica,
tornava dal cielo al beduino analfabeta.
Né tu, sultano, né il povero beduino,
avete pianto per una stella o una lucciola,
ma per la sola cosa per cui piange un uomo,
una donna: lì fu il dolore di luce persa,
premonizione astrale del tempo spegnente,
l'estinzione già inclusa nella ferita del miracolo,
e la distanza dal cielo, la morte.
Impara dal beduino, amala come si ama una lucciola,
donati a ogni istante di sopravvivenza,
e quando lei ti parrà persa nella notte
tu nei suoi occhi scoprirai di colpo
la luce alta delle stelle fisse,
e in lei che parve dissolversi in una notte d'agosto
l'affinità mortale con te che la supplichi.

LAURA STORTONI-HAGER

A native Italian, Laura Stortoni-Hager was brought up in Milan and received an international education and higher education degrees in the U.S. She has taught at major universities in Oregon and in Northern California. She has published two books of verse translations of Italian Renaissance women poets, *Gaspara Stampa: Selected Poems*, in 1994, and *Women Poets of the Italian Renaissance: Courtly Ladies and Courtesans*, in 1997. In 1996, she founded Hesperia Press for the promotion of modern Italian poetry in translation. She had translated into English and published the poetry of Maria Luisa Spaziani and Giuseppe Conte. In 1997 Stortoni published *The Moon and the Island*, her first volume of personal poetry, with a preface by Diane di Prima. She has also translated into Italian and published poetry in Italy by modern American poets, such as Lawrence Ferlinghetti, John Wieners and Diane di Prima. She makes her home in Berkeley, CA, and in Milan, Italy.

Laura Stortoni's poems are translated by the author.

How Could They?

How could my ancestors abandon those cities —
those cities of limestone and sun,
of Baroque intricacies in the wrought iron balconies,
and walls with caper plants
blooming in the cracks.
How could they allow
the silence to reclaim them?

Ships floated away from the coast
as on wide wings:
my people
scattered to the four directions —
as when the milkweed pod splits
flinging
white fluff to the winds.

As for me,
I do not know why I went away.
I was not moved by need.
I do not even know
if it was my heart's desire:
Fate and man's will
are two different things.

Now,
I look at the stars and I think of my land,
the land of the cactus people.
The same stars shine there,
the same moon.

My land, I think of you.
In my thoughts,
I caress you with flowers.

La terra dei fichidindia

Come hanno potuto i miei antenati abbandonare
queste città di tufo e di argilla,
con intricatezze barocche nelle ringhiere dei balconi
e pianti di capperi in fiore nelle crepe dei muri?

Perché hanno permesso al silenzio di riconquistarle?
Navi salpavano dai porti su grandi ali di vele.
La mia gente si è dispersa in tutte le direzioni
come polline al vento.

E io? Non so perché sono andata via.
Non so neanche se era quello che volevo.
Il fato e la volontà umana sono due cose diverse.

Ora guardo le stelle e penso alla mia terra, la terra
dei fichidindia. Mia terra, ti penso, nei miei pensieri
ti accarezzo con fiori profumati.

The Return

At night I look at the stars —
                    the Chaldean stars.

Under the tessellated sky
                    so much land-nothing but land —
trees of great shade, bushes and woods
              a splendor of spears
                              indigo and gold
                                    in the moonlight.
From this hemisphere
I have watched portents in the sky
                    eclipses biting at the sun.
In the middle of the moon,
              white sails that lull in water —
mountains that are no mountains.

Destiny has prodded me in all directions
since I came forth from my mother's womb.

I parted with my land for a while,
so that I would not be parted forever.

For sheaves of years
I have sifted the ashes of foreign lands.

Now my song
                    pierces like a knife:
I am one of the remembers.
We all come from somewhere
              and there we must return.

The sky pales: it is time.
I shall return to my land.
There is my ziggurat.

Il ritorno

Di notte guardo le stelle, le stelle caldee.
Sotto il cielo trapunto intravedo grandi pianure,
alberi di vasta ombra, boschi e folti cespugli:
uno splendore di lance indaco ed oro

al lume di luna. Da quest'emisfero ho osservato
portenti del cielo, eclissi che mordono il sole.
Nel mezzo della luna, vele bianche
che oscillano. Il destino mi ha spinto qui

da quando sono uscita dal grembo di mia madre.
Per fascine di anni ho setacciato le ceneri
di terre straniere. Ora il mio canto

trafigge come un coltello affilato. Il cielo
impallidisce. E'ora. Ritornerò nella mia terra.
E' là il mio ziggurat.

My grandfather's house

The big house my grandfather built,
with the white marble staircase and iron railings,
comes to my mind tonight. I was born upstairs,
in the old iron bed that now rusts in the attic.

My grandmother died a long time ago,
but her voice still echoes in my ears.
She knew I was a wild one,
"There now, *Lauruccia*, here is your little

embroidery hoop. Embroider just one little carnation."
But I roamed the Sicilian fields thinking of America,
dreaming of prairies wider than the whole island,

and a loneliness deeper than anything I could imagine.
And now I have it, loneliness,
and a garden of real pink carnations.

La grande casa di mio nonno

La grande casa che costruì mio nonno
con la scala di marmo e la ringhiera,
mi viene in mente stasera. Sono nata di sopra, nel letto
di ferro battuto che ora arrugginisce in soffitta.

Mia nonna è morta da tanto tempo,
ma le sue parole echeggiano nelle mie orecchie:
"Ecco, Lauruccia, ecco il tuo telaricchio.
Ricama, ricama un solo garofano rosso".

Sapeva che ero selvatica. Vagabondavo tra i campi
con la figlia del carrettiere. Sognavo l'America
e praterie più vaste dell'intera isola,
e una solitudine più profonda del pozzo della vigna.
E ora sono in America, e ce l'ho, la solitudine,
e un giardino di veri garofani rossi.

The Robber of Songs
From a Fragment of a Nahuatl Poem

Here I am!
I have come to sing:

Listen to my songs!
They are famous.
My renown grows and grows.

I fly!
I will fly as far as Panotla.
I come from the heart of Tula.
My voice
soars above you.

I make the flowers blossom!

Listen!
Listen to me carefully!

>   *I am a poet*
>   *I am a robber of songs*

Poet, how can you make them yours?
Draw some lines
red ... yellow ... blue ...
Draw them carefully.
When the songs have become yours
you will no longer suffer.

Il ladro di canti

> *Ispirato a un frammento di canto Nahuatl*

Ecco
vengo per cantare
Ascoltate
i miei canti!
Sono famosi
La mia fama
cresce sempre più
Volo
Volerò fino a Panotla
Vengo dal cuore di Tula
La mia voce
si libra sopra di voi
Faccio aprire i fiori!

Ascoltate!
Ascoltate con attenzione!
> *Sono un poeta*
> *Sono un ladro di canti*

Poeta, come li puoi rendere tuoi?
Disegna delle righe
rosse ... gialle ... blu ...
Disegnale con cura
Quando i canti saranno diventati tuoi
non soffrirai più

Let the Words Be Mine

There are women for whom duels are fought,
fleets are launched,
wars waged, armies massacred.
Others for whose beauty
homelands are forsaken,
children abandoned, thrones abdicated.
There are women for whom fortunes are amassed,
fortunes are lost. Others for whom
poems are written,
hymns are sung.

I want to wage my own war,
sing my own paean,
record my existence.

LET THE WORDS BE MINE!

May the reasons I am remembered
be my own deeds,
my own words.

Che le parole siano mie

Esistono donne per cui ci si batte a duello,
per cui si lanciano flotte,
si fanno guerre, si massacrano armate.
Altre per la cui bellezza
patrie sono abbandonate,
figli dimenticati, troni abdicati.
Esistono donne per cui si ammassano fortune,
si perdono fortune.
Altre per cui
si scrivono poesie,
si cantano inni.

Io
voglio combattere la mia guerra,
cantare il mio peana,
fare la cronaca della mia esistenza.

CHE LE PAROLE SIANO MIE!

Che le ragioni per cui sarò ricordata
siano le mie azioni,
le mie parole.

Kokopelli Makes the Sun Rise
Inspired by Pueblo mythology

I sleep in a fortress
My fortress
is a circle drawn on the sand

When I play the flute
the sky opens up
and bright yellow flowers
                    rain down on thorny cactus

I hang at the edge of sunshine

At daybreak

                    I rise
                    I go
                    I run
                    My bundle wants
                    to shake!

Last night I heard the Gods laugh
making a wide circle
                    around the moon

I open my way among the sagebrush
The face of the mountain
smiles at me: the mountain
                    tries to reach me
                              with her toes

Kokopelli fa sorgere il sole
Ispirato alla mitologia Pueblo

Dormo entro una fortezza
La mia fortezza
è un cerchio disegnato sulla sabbia

Quando suono il flauto
il cielo si apre
e fiori gialli e brillanti
            piovono dai cactus spinosi

Sono sospeso all'orlo
                della luce del sole

All'alba
        Sorgo
        Vado
        Corro
        La mia gobba
        vuole fare quattro salti!

Stanotte ho sentito gli dei che ridevano,
ridevano
danzando intorno alla luna

Mi apro la via tra i cespugli di salvia
Il viso della montagna
mi sorride: la montagna
                cerca di raggiungermi
                    con le dita dei piedi

I grab notes
and scatter them around
like pumpkin seeds

These mountains,
these valleys
are mine

The clouds dance to my tune

above my mountains
above my valleys

I stretch my hand out to the horizon

                    I AM THE EARTHQUAKE
                    I AM THE LIGHTNING

My song makes the Sky-Dwellers jealous

At daybreak I rise

                    I have done it!
                    I have woken up the sun!
                    I have made the sun rise!

Now I'll send swallows
blackbirds
and ravens
        to fly all
                over the desert

Afferro note
e le spargo intorno
come manciate di semi di zucca

Queste montagne,
queste vallate
sono mie.

Le nuvole danzano alla mia musica

sulle mie montagne
sulle mie valli

Stendo la mano all'orizzonte:

> IO SONO IL TERREMOTO!
> IO SONO IL FULMINE!

Il mio canto
ingelosisce gli abitanti del cielo

All'alba mi alzo,

> *Ci sono riuscito!*
> *Ho svegliato il sole!*
> *Ho fatto sorgere il sole!*

Ora
manderò sparvieri,
rondini e corvi
    a volare
    alti
        su tutto il deserto.

Penelope in the Third Decade

It was all a story, that about Fate
and the wrath of the Gods. The truth is, I bored him.
And as for me, I desired him to leave
as much as he desired it. He could never be still. Barely
had he returned than he started talking
about his next journey.
I did not mind: nobody is abandoned
who does not want to be, as well know the wives
of soldiers, sailors and of traveling merchants.

For many years, I lived by myself,
for nothing pleased me better
than to sleep alone, to own my body.
All called me, praised my fidelity. But I was not
faithful to *him*. I was faithful to *myself.*
I wove and unraveled, I twisted
threads of many colors into wondrous shapes —
and then, I unraveled them all.

> *We all make our fate, Odysseus, I thought,*
> *and you made yours of wanderer and adventurer.*
> *And I made mine of stable and prudent queen.*
> *We all make our fate, then blame the gods for it.*
> *Without knowing it, we had been well-paired:*
> *you, who always wanted to roam,*
> *and I, who always wanted to stay —*
> *we both had our freedom.*

Penelope racconta come sono andate veramente le cose

Era tutta una storia, quella del Fato e dell'ira degli dei.
In realtà, lo annoiavo. Quanto a me, desideravo che partisse,
quanto lui voleva partire. Non poteva mai stare fermo.
Appena tornato, già parlava del prossimo viaggio.
Non mi importava: nessuno è abbandonato
se non vuole essere abbandonato, come ben sanno le mogli
dei soldati di ventura, dei marinari e dei commessi viaggiatori.

Per molti anni, vissi da me. Mi piaceva dormire sola,
essere la sola padrona del mio corpo.
Tutti mi chiamavano casta, lodavano la mia fedeltà.
Ma non ero fedele a lui, ero fedele a me stessa.
Tessevo tele di mille colori: e poi le disfacevo.

Ognuno si fa il suo Fato, Odisseo.
Tu ti sei fatto il tuo di guerriero e di avventuriero,
e io il mio di stabile e prudente regina.
Tutti facciamo il nostro Fato, e poi biasimiamo gli dei.
Senza saperlo, eravamo stati ben accoppiati:
tu che volevi sempre partire, io che volevo sempre restare:
tutti e due avevamo la nostra libertà.

It pleased him to think that I waited for him with longing.
But I waited, if you can call it that, calmly,
enjoying life day by day: I had a child, a household,
a storeroom with *pithoi* filled with oil and grain,
an orchard with fig trees and pomegranates,
sweet hills covered with purple grapevines,
a garden where blue agapanthus seemed to soar.

A good life.
I understood that what is far is as near as near,
and near is as far as far,
and that no journey can be enjoyed
without the thought of the return.

And who is the hero? The one who departs? The one who stays?
Ultimately, they end up at the same place — and often,
the one who stayed has traveled
farther than the wanderer...
an inward journey.

It surprised him that I did not recognize him at first.
Recognize him I did, but I wanted to buy time.
He told me about the Nymph and the Sorceress,
how they had wanted him,
how they had tried to detain him...
Why did he tell me? I did not
ask. I did not care.
Again, I surrendered myself to him,
knowing that it would not be for long.

Si compiaceva di credere che lo aspettavo con ansia.
Aspettavo, se così si può dire, con calma, vivendo giorno per giorno.
Avevo un figlio, un regno, un palazzo, poderi, magazzini
di orci pieni d'olio e di grano, un frutteto di fichi e di melograni,
dolci colline coperte di vigne purpuree,
e un giardino dove i fiori dell'agapanto
si libravano più azzurri del cielo.
Una buona vita.

Capii che ciò che è lontano è più vicino di ciò che è vicino,
e che ciò che è vicino è più lontano di ciò che è lontano.
Che non si può intraprendere nessun viaggio
senza l'anticipazione del ritorno.

E poi, chi è l'eroe? Quello che parte? Quello che rimane?
Finiscono allo stesso posto, e spesso colui che è rimasto
ha viaggiato più lontano del viaggiatore:
un viaggio interno.

Fu sorpreso dal fatto che non lo riconobbi.
Ma lo avevo riconosciuto, solo, volevo guadagnare tempo.
Mi raccontò della Ninfa e della Maga, come lo avevano desiderato,
come lo avevano sedotto, come avevano tentato di trattenerlo...
Ma io non gli avevo chiesto niente.
Di nuovo mi arresi a lui, sapendo che non sarebbe stato per molto.

And the cycle began again. He left
on another adventure. This time,
never to come back.
It did not sadden me, for I was navigating
the seas of *my own* mind.

I was traveling
inside myself,
deeper and deeper…
until I found
what I had been looking for:
and what that is,
I will never tell
anyone.

E il ciclo cominciò di nuovo. Partì per un'ultima avventura,
questa volta per non tornare mai più.
Non mi rattristai, perché stavo navigando
i mari e gli oceani della mia mente.
Stavo viaggiando dentro me stessa sempre più profondamente.

Fino a quando trovai ciò che avevo cercato:
e quello che era,
non lo rivelerò mai a nessuno.

ROBERTO CARIFI

Roberto Carifi was born in Pistoia in 1949 where he lives and teaches Philosophy. He has published eight books of poetry. The last one, published in 1998, is entitled *L'amore d'autunno/Love in the Fall*. Roberto Carifi is a translator of German and French authors and has also published philosophical essays.

Roberto Carifi's poems are translated by Laura Stortoni-Hager.

***

In the West the ships are sinking. When?
Is it right, the voice that talks about nothingness?
They sparkle sometimes, but it is not the sun,
rather a fire, a bonfire lit in the night.
It happens in the West, only in the West
if hands give the order,
and the frightful gesture commands.
It is time to descend, to go sloping down
towards the mists, to drag oneself, if needed,
like dead souls looking for an exit:
these are the orders, it's final.
It's snow, the woman greeting the sailors,
snow that will melt round the corner,
that will be annihilated in secret,
when the embers of memories are kindled.
In the West those who don't sail are lost.

From *Occidente*

***

A occidente affondano le navi. Quando?
E' giusta la voce che racconta il nulla?
Scintillano, a volte, ma non è sole
piuttosto un fuoco, un fuocherello acceso nella notte.
Accade a occidente, soltanto a occidente
se danno l'ordine le mani
e comanda il gesto spaventoso.
E ora di scendere, degradare laggiú,
verso le nebbie, arrancare se occorre
come morti che cercano l'uscita:
questi sono gli ordini, poi basta.
E neve la donna che saluta i marinai;
si scioglierà dietro l'angolo,
si annullerà in segreto,
quando si accende la brace dei ricordi
a occidente è perduto chi non salpa.

***

Today nostalgia has found its tongue,
and words for my torment.
The rain hammers on the window panes
and the bell tolls.
The cat glides among my papers,
spying on my grieving soul.
What does a cat feel in her heart —
the same emptiness I feel,
the silence of love?
A shadow delineates itself on the wall —
perhaps it's the sunset, the dimmed lights —
but I hear crying, a lament fills the room.
To whom do you belong, tears? Whose voice is it?
Maybe the voices of poor, abandoned objects.
But, if they feel pain and memory wounds them,
they can silently retreat into nothingness. Like the angels they suffer
in another language, their crying is foreign to us.
Then we question them, as children do with their dolls,
we ask about them, if they have loves
or faults, if they feel remorse.
They remain silent; and we, lost to our voices.
Who is crying, whose lament is this?
It's already night, I think. Will it be definitive?
The shadow comes towards me, asks of us,
wonders where your glance is,
where my glance is, reduced to a desert.

***

Oggi la nostalgia ha trovato la sua lingua,
le parole al mio tormento.
La pioggia martella i vetri
e la campana suona a morto.
La gatta scivola tra le mie carte,
spia la mia anima dolente,
che cosa sente un gatto nel suo cuore,
lo stesso vuoto mio,
il silenzio dell'amore.
Un'ombra si disegna sopra il muro,
sarà il crepuscolo, le luci soffocate,
ma sento piangere, un lamento occupa la stanza.
A chi appartieni, pianto, di chi è la voce?
Saranno le cose povere, gli oggetti abbandonati.
Ma loro, se provano dolore e il ricordo li ferisce.
muti indietreggiano nel nulla. Come l'angelo soffrono
in un'altra lingua, il loro pianto per noi è straniero.
Allora li interroghiamo, come fanno i bambini
con le bambole, domandiamo di loro, se hanno amori
o colpe, se provano il rimorso.
Restano silenziosi, e noi smarriti nella nostra voce.
Chi piange, di chi è il lamento?
E già la notte, penso, sarà definitiva?
L'ombra mi viene incontro, chiede di noi,
domanda notizie del tuo sguardo,
notizie del mio ridotto a un deserto.

The voice has a familiar tone. I recognize you, death,
as a child you often spoke to me, near the tablecloth,
while your face was enveloped in shade.
A lantern sufficed to show you mine,
already devoid of smiles.
You, tears, who are always the same,
what do you ask of me?
What answer can there be to sobs?
I don't know, I too am an angel.
I cry alone in the shadow of God.

From *Amore e destino*

La voce ha un timbro familiare. Ti riconosco, morte,
da bambino mi parlavi spesso accanto alla tovaglia,
una penombra ti fasciava il viso.
Bastava una lucerna per mostrarti il mio,
già disertato dal sorriso.
Che mi domandi, pianto sempre uguale?
Cosa rispondere al singhiozzo?
Non so, sono un angelo anch'io,
piango da solo nell'ombra di Dio.

***

What will be of my life?
I ask you, unnamed light,
I ask you, sunset.
Will I be alien, excluded,
will I camp out where nothing grows,
where even memory is deserted?
Will I at least have a shelter for my tears,
where, silent, I can lock myself in memories?
I ask you, empty orbs of the night.

From *Amore e destino*

***

Che ne sarà della mia vita?
Te lo domando, luce innominabile
lo chiedo a te, crepuscolo.
Sarò straniero, espulso,
mi accamperò dove non cresce nulla,
dov'è deserta perfino la memoria?
Mi resterà almeno un alloggio per il pianto,
dove serrarmi muto nei ricordi?
Ve lo domando, orbite vuote della notte.

**

You know, love, that I take leave in haste,
that I touch the earth too lightly,
that my destiny lies in empty pockets
and in a naked angel that, at night,
cries livid on my breast.
And I pass under November's walls
with a message to carry
I don't know where, I don't know to whom,
written with sobs like a prayer.
I go almost fraternal in the night
looking for supervised shadows,
for certain lit lamps
and the extinguished eye of lost souls.

From *Amore e destino*

***

Lo sai, amore, che mi congedo in fretta,
che tocco terra con troppa leggerezza,
che ho un destino nelle tasche vuote
e un angelo spoglio che di sera
mi piange livido sul petto.
E passo sotto le mura di novembre
con un messaggio da portare
non so né a chi né dove,
scritto a singhiozzi come una preghiera,
e vado quasi fratello nella notte
guardando ombre sorvegliate,
certi lumini accesi
e l'occhio spento di anime perdute.

***

I am a poet, you see, I lift my beret up in the air
inside there is a heart that gives greetings,
a lightning that sets quickly —
and while I touch you, I think
that Autumn is a mournful soul.
I go away towards the invisible I love,
that moistens my chest.
I go away thinking I could make you happy,
if I didn't have an angel walking next to me.

From *Amore e destino*

***

Sono poeta, vedi, sollevo in aria il mio berretto,
dentro c'è un cuore che saluta,
un lampo che tramonta presto,
mentre ti sfioro penso
che l'autunno è un'anima dolente
e mi allontano verso quell'invisibile che amo
e che mi bagna il petto,
e mi allontano e penso che ti farei felice
se non avessi un angelo che mi cammina accanto.

***

I love those worn-out Madonnas,
those creatures lost in exile.
Sometimes at a street corner
an unknown shadow numbs me.
Hello, I say to her, my sister in frost!
And I go on
with an ancient tremor in my pen,
with a sob hidden in my hand —
and I know that a shiver of snow
will kiss my forehead.

From *Amore e destino*

***

Amo quelle madonne consumate
le creature perse in un esilio,
talvolta a un angolo di strada
mi rattrappisce un'ombra sconosciuta.
Salve, ti dico, sorella mia nel gelo!
E vado, e vado
con un tremore antico nella penna
con un singhiozzo stretto nella mano
e so che un brivido di neve
mi bacerà la fronte.

TOMASO KEMENY

Tomaso Kemeny was born in Budapest in 1939 and presently lives in Milan. He is a professor of English literature at the University of Pavia. He has published five books of poetry. The last one, in 1998, is entitled *Melody*. Since 1985 Tomaso Kemeny has worked on an epic poem that will be published next year. He is one of the founders of the movement of *Mitomodernismo* and is also the translator of the poetry of Lord Byron and many other poets. Tomaso Kemeny is also the author of critical essays.

Tomaso Kemeny's poems are translated by Laura Stortoni-Hager.

Prologue

I sing of the eagle in flight
before the skies were created;
I sing of the flight that in the void
had shaped the tree and the snow-covered
branches before the mount arose
guarding the storm-whipped plains.
With my temple grizzled in the rage
of the extreme love's season,
I sing of the blood as red
as the sun that rose in the beginning
dissolving the thick darkness
in the glory of the first morning.
I sing of the river that flows
forever beyond the space barriers
and enters the mournful whirl of time
when man's frail cosmos
is hurled into the orbit of the skull,
titanic abode of the soul.
(I do not sing the blind night
of the pusher revved up
and insensitive
to the miserable pierced
by the lights of the proud cities
and broken off in the garbage.)
In the uproar of the unbounded surge I listen
to Tasso's voice sublime
whose echo drives out of my mind
all that's superfluous and brings the soul
into the austere, solemn and resonating
cathedral of poetic faith.

Prologo

Canto l'aquila in volo
prima che fossero creati i cieli;
canto il volo che figurò nel vuoto
l'albero e i rami innevati
prima che sorgesse monte a presidio
delle piane frustate dall'uragano.
Le tempie brizzolate nella furia
dell'estrema stagione amorosa,
canto il sangue vermiglio
come il sole che sorse in principio
dissolvendo la tenebra compatta
nella gloria del primo mattino.
Canto il fiume che scorre da sempre
oltre le barriere dello spazio
e varca il gorgo luttuoso del tempo
allorché il cosmo fragile dell'uomo
s'inabissa nell'orbita del teschio,
titanica dimora dell'anima.
(Non canto la notte cieca
del trafficante su di giri
insensibile agli sballati trafitti
dalle luci delle città orgogliose
e troncati nell'immondezza).
Nel fragore delle grandi acque ascolto
la voce sublime del Tasso
la cui eco scaccia dalla mente
il superfluo e trasmuta l'anima
nell'austera, solenne e risonante
cattedrale della fede poetica.

I slip into a linen tunic
and I see a host of cherubim
dilate the ashes of dreams
in the likeness of the starry vault
where Urania does count the names
of the dead Magyar captains
and sings of the deeds of those
who lived fighting for Transylvania.
My voice discovers the astral bodies
and among the clouds it raises ruins
and shatters the monuments to the invader
and debars its gestures from the visible,
that only in front of the oppressed
the gates of the temple open wide.
I sing of the courage that draws
heaven and earth together, I follow
the eagle in flight
to the burning ring of the sun
so that with the clay of the river
which flows beyond the whirls of death
I may shape the marvellous God invoked
by those who fight for beauty
and for the glow of the origins.

Indosso una tunica di lino
e vedo una schiera di cherubini
dilatare la cener dei sogni
a immagine della volta stellata
dove Urania enumera i nomi
dei defunti capitani magiari
e canta le gesta di chi visse
combattendo per la Transilvania.
La mia voce ritrova i corpi astrali
e tra le nuvole innalza le rovine
e frantuma monumenti all'invasore
e i suoi gesti esclude dal visibile
perchè solo davanti agli oppressi
si spalanchi il portale del tempio.
Canto il coraggio che unisce
cielo e terra e seguo l'aquila in volo
verso il cerchio cocente del sole
per plasmare con l'argilla del fiume
che scorre oltre i gorghi della morte
il Dio portentoso invocato
da chi combatte per la bellezza
e per il bagliore delle origini.

Canto I (vv. 50-89)

. . . in the light of the new
world I saw the stone colossus
that holds in his left hand
the table of national independence
and with his right one raises
the torch of freedom to the sky.
93 metres of mirage
were hurled down the furious
sky because rarely
freedom skims over
the earth, perhaps only
when whoever craves for it
cannot live without fighting for it.
I was not in Budapest
with the machine-gun raised to the sky
nor did I kneel down
on the tombs of the patriots; I was
not there — I had long been
in the west — I was not there to fight for
the real independence;
nor did I block up with mud the periscope
of the tanks to open the way
for my brothers' molotov-cocktails.
I did not embellish my arm
with the National Guard tricolour, nor
did I see the teacherous Russians bury
in a flow of steel the cry
of freedom that saved a whole
people from dishonour.
I was not arrested, examined,
beaten up, interred in chains.

Canto I (vv. 50-89)

... Nella luce del mondo
nuovo vidi il colosso di pietra
che nella mano sinistra sorregge
la tavola dell'indipendenza nazionale
e con la destra alza verso il cielo
la fiaccola della libertà.
93 metri di miraggio
precipitarono nel cielo acceso
di collera poiché la libertà
sfiora solo di rado
la terra, forse solo
quando chi l'ama alla follia non sa
più vivere senza battersi per lei.
Io a Budapest non c'ero a salutare
con il mitra al cielo alzato
la ritirata dei carri armati,
né alla luce fioca dei lumini
m'inginocchiai sulle tombe
dei patrioti; non c'ero
da tempo in occidente
a battermi per l'indipendenza reale;
né accecai col fango il periscopio
dei carri per aprire la via
alle molotov dei miei compagni.
Non ornai il braccio col tricolore
della Guardia Nazionale, né vidi
a tradimento i Russi seppellire
in una colata d'acciaio il grido
di libertà che salvò un popolo
intero dal disonore.
Non fui arrestato, interrogato,
bastonato, inumato in catene.

But I am still here to listen
to the soldiers' voice
who in another November
paraded under the windows
of my father singing
"Sweet Transylvania, to You we come,
for You we live, for You we die."

Ma sono ancora qui ad ascoltare
la voce dei soldati
che in un altro novembre
sfilarono sotto le finestre
della dimora paterna cantando
'Dolce Transilvania, da Te veniamo,
per Te viviamo, per Te moriamo'.

Canto IV (vv. 10-47)

Unheard Harmony, Edith,
does not choose between knowledge and love,
her spirit vibrates in the hedge
of the drop of blood
and disavows the abyss
that decrepit unfolds
the coil around the globe.
She has never gone that high,
beyond every living
form, her eyes
glide over the world like ocean
returning the dead.
The sun is a fire wound
in the forest of the tears
where the fallen man
gets lost in the dawn.
"Dear Anyu, mother sweet, sing
once more the thyme
scented plain,
far and odorous
with the milk of the smoke-and-wind
mares, the Prince's tent
beyond the Glass Mountain,
the burning chair of the shamans,
the seven seals that answer for
the truth on this side of the golden woods,
the corn poppies that bud free
at the shout of the fiery oak wood ..."

Canto IV (vv. 10-47)

Armonia Inaudita, Edith,
tra conoscenza e amore non sceglie,
il suo spirito vibra nella siepe
della goccia di sangue
e ripudia l'abisso
che si disvolge decrepito
per attorcigliarsi intorno al globo.
Non è mai salita tanto in alto,
al di là di ogni forma
vivente, il suo sguardo
scorre sul mondo come oceano
che restituisce i morti.
Il sole è una piaga di fuoco
nella foresta di lacrime dove
l'uomo caduto
si perde nell'aurora.
"Cara Anyu", soave madre, cantami
ancora la pianura
profumata di timo,
lontana e fragrante
del latte delle cavalle di fumo
e di vento, la tenda del Principe
al di là della Montagna di Vetro,
l'ardente coro degli sciamani,
i sette sigilli che garantiscono
il vero al di qua dei boschi d'oro,
i rosolacci che sbocciano liberi
al grido del querceto focoso..."

Leviathans raise
their manes and the brazen
and golden books melt
into the secret
consumption of symbols
until Edith's soul
nocturnal is born again
within the circle of perfection
traced on the unexpiable
void of the origins.

From *La Transilvania Liberata* (unpublished)

Leviatani alzano
criniera e i libri
di bronzo e di oro si fondono
nella cosumazione
segreta dei simboli
finchè l'anima di Edith
notturna non rinasce
nel cerchio della perfezione
tracciato sul vuoto inespirabile
delle origini.

MARIO BAUDINO

Mario Baudino was born in 1952, lives in Turin and writes for *La stampa*, a prestigious national newspaper. He has published two books of poems: *Una regina tenera e stupenda/A Beautiful and Loving Queen* and *Grazie/Thanks*. A third one is coming out this year: *Colloqui con un vecchio nemico/Conversations with an Old Enemy*. Baudino has also published essays and two novels: *In volo per affari/Flying for Business* in 1994 and *Il sorriso della druida/The Mmile of the Druid Priestess* in 1998, a story about Celtic heritage in Northern Italy.

Mario Baudino's poems are translated by Laura Stortoni-Hager.

Entrusted to the voice

Fear, trust, insanity
he said, and the fourth word was pain
the fifth nothing, and at that point
he paused as if stumbling, as
if the radio had just gone off
after hours of buzzing and buzzing
racing with the tape recorder

From *Colloqui con un vecchio nemico*

Affidato alla voce

paura, fiducia, follia
disse, e la quarta parola era dolore
la quinta nulla e lì
ebbe un indugio come inciampando, come
se fosse stata spenta ora la radio
che ronzava ronzava già da ore
correndo col registratore

***

I don't know if he is happy
whether the evening breeze brings him
hoards of daydreams
or if perhaps he stares a little at the clouds
moving with the rhythm of the birds, if

it rains inside his soul
if there is a room
washed out by the smell of dust,
and dampness and leaves, as when
the first drop has already fallen
and you have never seen it, never

***

non so se sia contento
se il soffio della sera gli porti
battaglioni di sogni ad occhi aperti
o se magari guardi un poco nubi
muoversi al ritmo dei pennuti, se

piova nel suo interno
d'anima, se ci sia una stanza
dilavata dall'odore di polvere
e d'umido e foglie, come quando
la prima goccia è già caduta e mai
mai una volta che tu l'abbia veduta

***

It is often repeated,
with a certain joy
as if it had never happened to her
never happened to him:
Yes, yes, I want to be myself

Silence, I would tell her not knowing
if the voice is a lost soul
perhaps mine

Silence, I would tell her not knowing
if she had only let herself go,
silence, you don't know,
I would tell her, foolish
daughter of time, daughter of the wheel

What a bore before you die

***

Lo ripete spesso, con
una certa gioia,
come se mai non gli fosse
non le fosse successo: sì, sì
voglio essere me stesso

Taci, le direi non sapendo se sia
quella voce un'anima sperduta
forse la mia

Taci, le direi non sapendo se si sia
soltanto abbandonata
taci, non sai, le direi anima idiota
figlia del tempo figlia della ruota

non sai che noia
prima che tu muoia

***

The first man who sold her
she doesn't remember him
all the others were alike
but this is not what matters

The first one smiled, perhaps
but it was a brief affair
in life it's important to endure
sensible shoes and a coat

Clothes should be comfortable, at least
in the mist:
she has not been able to smell for a long time
smoke a sigarette and toil!

***

Il primo che la vendette
non lo ricorda
gli altri si somigliavano tutti
non è questo che conta

Il primo sorrise, forse
ma fu un affare da poco
nella vita l'importante è durare
scarpe comode e un paltò

Siano le vesti affidabili, almeno
nella nebbia:
gli odori non li sente più da molto tempo
fuma una sigaretta e sgobba

***

He didn't know a greater sweetness in himself
nor anything else listed among the paragraphs
of a love canon
He just gave up his loins to sadness
to the macumba of loneliness

The demon of hours runs winged
the angel of the diary

He didn't want a greater fullness in himself
this sense of duty
gave him pleasure

Winged runs the demon of order
the blindfolded angel

***

Non sapeva di sé maggior dolcezza
né altro annoverato tra i paragrafi
d'un canone d'amore
consegnò le sue reni alla tristezza
alla macumba della solitudine

Alato corre il demone delle ore
l'angelo dell'agenda

Non voleva di sé maggior pienezza
il senso del dovere
gli faceva piacere

Alato corre il demone dell'ordine
l'angelo con la benda

***

He loved a shadow, he understood
that he was unfaithful
to dawn

He loved a shadow, yes
he said, this is the best way to love
(she was mobile and dull, she
was perfect in this regard)

He loved a shadow, so
he had nothing more to think about
it was enough for him to see her return
from time to time

***

Amò un'ombra, capì
che era infedele
all'alba

Amò un'ombra, sì
disse, è questo il modo d'amare
più corretto (lei
era mobile e scialba, era
perfetta, sotto questo aspetto)

Amò un'ombra, così
non ebbe più da pensare
gli bastava vederla
qualche volta tornare

***

to try to think of her, to sink
into the color of the trees at night
or in the slothful indigo of dawn
and it is not enough
to try to tempt her, to ask her
politely if her slight presence can
give you a personal experience
to try a pattern, like
the noise of thoughts at night
the smell of a cigar
what remains and flies about.
only the cat stares at you
will it be like this, you ask him
or perhaps
even less, will it be
a crazy run

***

provare a pensarla, affondare
nel colore che hanno gli alberi di notte
o nell'indaco accidioso del mattino
e non basta
provare a tentarla, chiederle
per piacere se può la sua sparuta
presenza darti un'esperienza vissuta
provare un modello, come
il rumore che hanno i pensieri la notte
il profumo del sigaro
ciò che resta e svolazza
solo il gatto ti guarda
sarà così, gli chiedi
o forse
ancor meno, sarà
una corsa pazza

Letter

I don't know if you wanted from me news
or if you like the style
perhaps a little affected and uselessly
obsolete, with that marching pace, towards what
you ask me, I prefer
to try telling you from where, here, in the eves
of everything, in these rich
villages where windows are glowing
and we are smiling, and it seems
possibile to see, to hear, to touch
chips of real happiness, don't smile
if by chance you still have a mouth
a set of teeth (and they were
nice and rythmed, they used to make
some sort of gentle music, when your tongue,
your lips used to slide over them, or was it the tip
of a sigarette without filter) no, don't smile
if by chance something
remains, and I'm not really sure
I don't know if there is anything
to remember, eyes
hands, breath, voices, and I'm not really sure:
your answering machine was speaking about you
for another day, saying:
don't hang up!

Lettera

Se volessi mie nuove non so
e neppure se apprezzi la forma
forse un poco affettata e inutilmente
desueta, con quel passo di marcia, verso che
mi chiedi, preferisco
provare a dirti da dove, qui, nelle vigilie
di tutto, in questi ricchi
paesi dove brillano finestre
e sorridiamo e pare
di vedere sentire toccare
schegge di vera
felicità, non ridere
caso mai ti rimanga una bocca
una chiostra di denti (erano belli
molto ritmati, loro, e facevano
una sorta di musica lieve, quando
li sfioravi con la lingua, le labbra o il fondo
di una sigaretta senza filtro) no non ridere
caso mai qualcosa
rimanga, e non è che ne sia certo
né so se poi qualcosa
resti da ricordare, occhi
mani fiato voci, e non è che ne sia certo:
per qualche giorno ancora
parlava di te la tua segreteria
un nastro registrato che diceva: non riattaccate

It's easy to remember
everybody can manage it
this isn't the real burden
the train of the hours softly passes through and
I think that it is the lack
of gravity to reveal its horizon
to sentiment. Here
the heart's vessels row strongly
nevertheless there is a lot of wind, sometimes
a cloud clears up, as if it were
normal. Everything here is normal
the day, the snow, the horror
If you don't believe it, I don't know how to convince you
I have no proof

If you don't believe it, it will be an act of love
to expose all this
heroism of defeated resistants
of panting winners, you know how ravenous
the head of the pack is often
he barks all alone, often dealing out a volley of blows he puts
dreams in order, to each a name
mine changes so often, I'm the worst in my class
for a longtime I have no right to a content

If you don't believe it, I don't know how to convince you
I'm stuttering over the most difficult words
not longer, not yet, then, now
but here the night comes earlier and earlier.
He who can listen sometimes wins a prize.
It grabs you and devours you

Ricordare è facile, ci si riesce
il peso non è questo
passa leggero il treno delle ore, e credo
che sia l'assenza
di gravità a svelare al sentimento
il suo orizzonte. Qui
remano vigorose le navi del cuore
c'è molto vento d'altra parte e a volte
s'apre una nuvola come se poi fosse
normale. Qui è tutto normale
il giorno, la neve, l'orrore
se non ci credi non so come convincerti
non ne ho le prove

Se non ci credi sarà un atto d'amore
il mettere per strada tutto questo
eroismo di vinti resistenti
di vincitori ansanti, sai quant'è famelico
il capo-branco, spesso urla da solo, spesso a botte
fa ordine tra i sogni a ognuno un nome
il mio cambia sovente, sono
l'ultimo della classe, non ho avuto
da tempo più diritto a un contenuto
Se non ci credi non so come convincerti
balbetto le parole più difficili
non più, non ancora, poi, ora
ma qui la notte arriva sempre più presto
chi sa ascoltare a volte vince un premio:
ti prende e ti divora

MASSIMO A. MAGGIARI

Massimo Maggiari was born in Genova in 1960 and lives now in Charleston, South Carolina. He teaches Italian language and literature at the College of Charleston, where he organizes intercultural exchanges between Italian and American poets. He specialized in twentieth-century Italian poetry writing a critical study on Arturo Onofri and has published several articles, essays and reviews in Italian and American journals. Massimo Maggiari has published one book of poetry: *Terre lontane/Lands Away*.

Massimo Maggiari's poems are translated by Laura Stortoni-Hager.

The invisible Fjord

Wind, you who blow
down from the mountain tops,
breathe in the song
of the wheat
and refresh the sea
with the youth of the hillsides.

Sow
the summits of the world
scratch and push forward
celestial dreams
in the steps and the faces
of the new dawn.

Sow
the sluggishness of summer
and whisper slowly
"I, too, am dying"
like the vines waiting for September
"I, too, am moaning"
there among stars and horizons
devoid of sun, kindled by moonlight
pure salt down there
in the brackish furrow
of a thousand silvery graves.

I listen between wave and myth
in the deepest birth of your name
I find again the blood of the dead
the steps of the sled hounds
the scattered voices of the Pole.

L'invisibile fiordo

Vento che soffi
dall'alto dei monti
respira il canto
del grano saraceno
e affresca il mare
della gioventù dei colli.

Semina tu,
altezze di mondo
e afferra e spingi
i sogni celesti
nei passi e i volti
del nuovo mattino.

Semina tu,
la lentezza estiva
e sussurra dolcemente
"anch'io sto morendo"
come le viti che aspettano settembre
"anch'io sto gemendo"
laggiù tra stelle e orizzonti
spento di sole acceso di luna
salsedine pura laggiù
nel solco salmastro
con mille fosse d'argento.

Accolto tra onda e mito
nel parto più fitto del tuo nome
ritrovo il sangue dei morti
i passi dei cani da slitta
le voci disperse del Polo.

You are Amundsen, the explorer
the lord of the invisible fjord.

You live and make others live

At your passing
the glaciers
wait for the summer
and the winds
the hot winds of autumn —
breathe in the sun
and the solitary harvest.

Tu sei Amundsen, l'esploratore
signore dell'invisibile fiordo

tu vivi, e fai vivere

al tuo passare i ghiacci
aspettano l'estate
e i venti
i caldi venti dell'autunno
respirano sole
e raccolto solitario.

Towards the Big Dipper

They fluctuate, mobile, in the body of life
and like streamers they surface
in dances of embrace and flight.

They watch the skies and the earth
and navigate slow, silent,
while the beating heart
opens their faces wide
to the four directions
of the world.

Sunk are the paradises
of the ether,
the plastic marvels
of the shapeless cities.
The gods of sleep
freshen up faces
made of silk and light,
and the Big Dipper's darts
beckon to the cosmos.

At the horizon, at the horizon
souls of the fjord,
what do you see?

In Nobile's nocturnal thoughts,
in Amundsen's mercurial steps,
in Shakelton's solar rescues,
what humanity is there ?

What destiny ?

Verso l'Orsa Maggiore.

Fluttuano mobili nel corpo di vita
e come astri filanti affiorano
in danze d'abbraccio e volo.

Scrutano i cieli e la terra
e navigano lenti silenziosi
mentre il cuore che batte
spalanca i visi
nelle quattro direzioni
del mondo.

Affogati i paradisi
degli eteri
e le meraviglie plastiche
delle città informi
gli dei del sonno
affrescano i volti
di luce e seta
e segnalano al cosmo
gli strali dell'Orsa Maggiore.

A vista, a vista
voi, anime del fiordo
che vedete?

Nei pensieri notturni di Nobile
nei passi mercuriali di Amundsen
nelle gesta solari di Shackleton,
quale umanità?

                    Quale destino?

The red tent collapses
at the center of the icecap,
rotating around itself
to the left, to the right
then sinks
in a dancing vortex,
its belly welcoming
chrysalides of butterflies.

From the thick of the eddy
emerges a mosaic of souls and wolves
and barefoot on the bodies of snow
a Portuguese little girl
hangs the Big Dipper's lights
over the mountain wings.

La tenda rossa sprofonda
al centro dei ghiacci
rotea su se stessa
di qua, di là
e in danza
accoglie nel ventre
crisalidi di farfalla.

Nel morso della risacca
emerge un mosaico
di anime e lupi
e scalza sui corpi di neve
una bambina portoghese
appende sull'ala dei monti
i bagliori dell'Orsa Maggiore.

Nobile in flight
"To the Pole, to the Pole!"
cry the warriors
and the rainbow's bridges
ask the thunder
for a peace of rain and snow.

"To the Pole, to the Pole!"
cry the warriors
and from the lands of Thule
come riding clouds and hearts
as far as the seven silvery summits.

"To the Pole, to the Pole!"
Do not tarry, rush
to the emperor's palace
and knock, knock
at the doors of grass and leaves
at the windows of rock and rice.
Knock till you are exhausted:
this is the gate
to the four kingdoms of the world.

Conquer the dragon!
Perform the magic gesture.
Make the flags shine blue
on the ice cap.
Free from salt
walk on the water's reflection
Dance, rejoice, forget.
Pull his teeth out
forever.

Red you shall be, pomegranate on the hill.

Nobile in volo
Al Polo, al Polo
gridano i guerrieri
e i ponti d'arcobaleno
chiedono al tuono la pace
di pioggia e neve.

Al Polo, al Polo
gridano i guerrieri
e dalle terre di Thule
cavalcano nubi e cuori
fino alle sette cime d'argento.

Al Polo, al Polo
non indugiate, presto
alla dimora dell'Imperatore
e bussate, bussate
alle porte di vetro e foglie
alle finestre di roccia e riso
bussate, fino a stremare:
questo è il cancello
dei quattro regni del mondo.

Vincete il drago
compite il gesto magico
inazzurrate le bandiere
sulla calotta di ghiaccio
camminate sui riflessi dell'acqua
liberi dalla salsedine
danzate, gioite, dimenticate
strappategli i denti
per sempre

rossi sarete melograno sui colli.

Amundsen's Paean

Wind, you who rise
dreams from the mountains,
breathe love and song
on the celestial bulwarks.
Offer
words and blood
to the voices of the world.

Protect my sky
my constellations
and their unborn stars.
Defend my fjord
and the scattered tribes
of the She-Bear's Hunters.

I am Roald Engelbert Amundsen
artic explorer, Norwegian by birth
I am the son of Iems,
builder of tall ships.
I come from Borge in Ostfold
I am the dreamer of the Big Dipper.

My body is a millenary tree.
I am strong, I am joyful.
I am wave, I am stone.
In the summer I have forty thousand branches.
In the winter I have eleven fingers.
In my dreams I catch the mind
in a sea of spray and silence.

Il peana di Amundsen

Vento che albeggi
i sogni dei monti
alita amore e canto
sugli spalti celesti
e offri
parole e sangue
alle voci del mondo.

Proteggi il mio cielo
le mie costellazioni
i loro astri nascenti
difendi il mio fiordo
e le sparse tribù
dei cacciatori dell'Orsa.

Io sono Roald Engelbert Amundsen
esploratore artico, norvegese
sono figlio di Iems
costruttore di velieri altissimi
di Borge nell'Ostfold
sognatore dell'Orsa Maggiore.

Ho un corpo d'albero millenario
sono forte, sono gioioso
sono onda e sasso
d'estate ho quarantamila rami
d'inverno ho undici dita
e in sogno afferro la mente
in un mare di spruzzi e silenzio.

I speak from my chest
in a language of tortoises and gulfs
while serene the mornings catch fire
offering the ships
a peace made of light and salt.

In the winter
of the year one thousand nine hundred and three
on King William's Island
at sunset
I boarded a little hull.
The Eskimos
could hear my steps
resound lightly
among the gorges of the fjords
to fade
in crystalline shadows.

At night I glided among the ice packs
immersed in pitch and mist
and the moon
that diffused milk-white light
looked for me in vain,
weaving at the helm
a thousand silvery flakes.

In secret with fire I cut
a northwest passage,
and in the melting glaciers
danced angels and black eyes.

Parlo dal petto
un lingua di tartarughe e golfi
e sereni i mattini s'incendiano
offrendo alle navi
una pace di luce e sale.

Nell'inverno del millenovecentotre
sull'isola di re Guglielmo
ai tramonti
salivo su un piccolo scafo
e gli esquimesi
sentivano i miei passi
leggeri risonare
tra le gole dei fiordi
e perdersi
nelle ombre di cristallo.

Le notti scivolavo tra le banchise
immerso tra pece e bruma
e la luna
che innevava di latte
invano mi cercava
filando al timone
mille fiocchi d'argento.

In segreto intagliavo di fuoco
un passaggio a nord-ovest
e nei ghiacci in fusione
danzavano occhi e angeli neri.

Terra Australis Incognita

Through Drake's sea
through its infinite waves
steering by the path of the stars
I have followed you, my soul,
for a thousand nights and a thousand winters,
and my voice has sailed with the silence.

As far as the eternal ices, as far as the ice banks
where the polar bear lives the long morning
I have followed you, my soul,
crying out to dreams
begging mercy
from the sky's rainbows.

Who are you? Whom do you sail with?
Where do you take us?

At every equinox
like an omen you appear in the sky
and the fresh air conjures deities
from the surface of the sea.

At every equinox
my dogs smell your passage
the night, tearing the day apart
and their blood speaks forests and death.

I will follow my dogs as far as tha Austral Pole
I will follow their destiny of bone and salt
I will melt your doors of ice
I will knock day and night
I will wait for dawn:
among the flames, among the flames
your face, your face.

Terra Australe Incognita

Per il mare di Drake
per le sue onde infinite
osservando il cammino delle stelle
ti ho inseguito, anima mia
mille notti e mille inverni
e la voce mia salpava il silenzio.

Fino ai ghiacci eterni, fino alle banchise
dove l'orso polare vive il lungo mattino
ti ho inseguito, anima mia
lanciando grida ai sogni
chiedendo pietà
agli arcobaleni del mondo.

Chi sei? Con chi navighi? Dove ci porti?

Ogni equinozio
appari nei cieli come un presagio
e l'aria fresca agita numi
sulla superficie del mare.

Ogni equinozio
i miei cani sentono il tuo passaggio
la notte e sbranano il giorno
e il loro sangue parla di foreste e di morte.

Seguirò i miei cani fino al Polo Australe
seguirò il loro destino di ossa e sale
scioglierò le tue porte di ghiaccio
busserò notte e giorno
aspetterò l'alba:
tra le fiamme, tra le fiamme
il tuo volto, il tuo volto.

The Celestial City

Distant and vague
to the blue skies
waters fly
to the expanses of the world
to the eddies of mud and rock
to the sources of light and bodies
Waters fly
from the flowing lights of the Great Bear.

Waters
to my coral heart
Waters
to my forty-two dogs
to my crystal sled
to the mountains with a thousand peaks
Waters, waters flying
in the stellar passes of the nocturnal sky.

Warriors of the Bear,
Forward! Do not tarry!
Sing Amundsen's exploits fervently
to the maiden of the fjord.

Rise on thin waters
free from the land of glass
towards the celestial city
beyond the pyre, beyond the sleep
of infinite days.

La città celeste

Lontane e vaghe
agli azzurri
volano acque
alle distese del mondo
agli abissi di fango e roccia
alle fonti di luci e corpi
volano acque
dai fluenti lumi dell'Orsa Maggiore.

Acque
al mio cuore di corallo
acque
ai miei quarantadue cani
alla mia slitta di cristallo
alle montagne dalle mille punte
acque, acque che volano
nei passi stellari del cielo notturno.

Guerrieri dell'Orsa
avanti, non indugiate
ferventi cantate
alla fanciulla del fiordo
le imprese di Amundsen
e cavalcate su acque sottili
liberi dalle terre di vetro
verso la città celeste
oltre il rogo, oltre il sonno
dei giorni infiniti.

Swarm far away
in the dances of the flames
on the mountain summits
Fly between moon and sun
Inhabit the sky, walk the earth.

And at night,
at night snow down
like souls
on the crevasses of autumn.

Sciamate lontano
nelle danze dei fuochi
sulle cime dei monti
volate tra luna e sole
abitate i cieli, camminate la terra

e la notte
la notte nevicate
come anime
sui crepacci d'autunno.

Inuit

Silver shadows
come forth
between silence and thunder
on flaming ridges
from lights and mountain passes
light shadows
glide away
on deserts rippled with ice.

On the crests
I see their bows
move like wolf bites,
scratch my heart in their run.

I lift my arms
and I cry to the fjords
the names of my dead
and the dawns of the world
cast imprints
on the evening voices.

Inuit brothers,
give my heart
the dawn of the day,
give the moon
the warmth of the night
cast sparks
to the memories of our fathers
and lift,
lift dreams and wings
to the soft hues
of the winter mantles.

Inuit

Ombre d'argento
che avanzano
tra silenzio e tuono
su creste infiammate
da luci e passi
ombre leggere
che scivolano via
su deserti increspati di ghiaccio.

Ai crinali
vedo i loro archi
muoversi come morsi di lupo
e in corsa graffiare il mio cuore.

Alzo le braccia
e grido ai fiordi
i nomi dei miei morti
e le aurore del mondo
scagliano impronte
sulle voci della sera.

Fratelli Inuit,
donate al mio cuore
l'alba del giorno
e alla luna
il calore della notte
gettate scintille
ai ricordi dei nostri padri
e alzate
alzate sogni e ali
ai soffici azzurri
dei manti d'inverno.

ROSITA COPIOLI

Rosita Copioli is one of the most renown exponent of *Mitomodernismo*. She lives in Rimini and has published poetry, essays and fiction. Her latest book of poetry is entitled *Elena/Helen*. She is a Yeats' scholar and translator. Although Copioli could not partecipate in person, she offered the following contribution.

Rosita Copioli's poems are translated by Laura Stortoni-Hager.

Distant Demon

I cannot, demon, sustain your glance.
What glance.
The most attractive eyes.

Demon, you who can empty even the void,
you trace streets of sorrow in every fiber,
you turn many masks, given and heavvy,
into the crystal that weakens
the happy water that slides from your eyes
to freeze into your heart.

Eye of mine, distant demon,
how happy was the way of our heart
before time thrust its clutches
into this terror.

Demon, you who before were
a width, a height, an apex of roses
and you have wanted to sedate it, shrink it, freeze it
in the astragalus—the holes of fate for its glance.

Demone remoto

Non posso, demone, sostenere il tuo sguardo.
Quale sguardo.
Occhi i più attraenti.

Demone che svuoti perfino il vuoto
tracci strade di dolore in ogni fibra
troppe maschere date e grevi
tramuti nel cristallo che punge-fiacca
l'acqua felice che scivola dagli occhi
e si gela nel cuore.

Occhio mio demone remoto
quanto felice la via del nostro cuore
prima che il tempo ficcasse l'artiglio
in questo terrore.

Demone che prima eri
una larghezza, un'altezza, un culmine di rose
e l'hai voluto sedare restringere gelare
nell'astragalo i buchi della sorte per suo sguardo.

Eleusis

Do not seek at Eleusis the sacred street of the cavern
that had a body and soul, Persephone.
Walls of scrap-iron, the rust
in the palaces, the gray houses, take you
to other abysses, sending signals
with the cloths at the windows.
You only look down that hole
that is planted down there, that can
suck your eyes like the eye
of a marine eddy. Ochre and black
and azure. That changes the colors into spirals. Narrow chasm,
round fissure of a well shaped like a body,
with rings of tufa and lips
for its walls. There were those who descend into it.
And now, by the thousands,
bubbles of red silk sails, puffed up by the
April sun agitate its mouth, animated
by the wind of the gulf; poppies pushed
to climb between sea and sky, expelled
by waves and more waves. The earth torn apart
by love, by pomegranate water, entrusts them
to the air; born impalpable, eyelids
of the nights devoted to the dawn.

Eleusi

Non cercare ad Eleusi la strada
sacra della caverna che ebbe,
anima e corpo, Persefone.
Muri di ferraglia, le ruggini
ai palazzi, le case grigie ti
portano ad altri abissi, lanciando
segnali coi panni delle finestre.
Tu mira soltanto quel buco
che si pianta in giù, che ti
risucchia gli occhi come l'occhio
di un gorgo marino. Ocra e nero
e azzurro. Che muta a spirali
i colori. Voragine stretta, rotonda
fessura di pozzo a misura di un corpo,
con anelli di tufo e labbra,
per sue pareti. Ci fu chi lo
scese. Ed ora, a mille e a mille
bolle di vele di seta rossa, gonfie del sole
d'aprile agitano la sua bocca, animate
da un vento di golfo; papaveri spinti
a salire tra cielo e mare, espulsi
da onde, e da onde. La terra squarciata
d'amore, d'acqua di melograna, li affida
all'aria: impalpabili nati, palpebre delle
notti devote all'aurora.

Heloise's Island

At the mouth of the Loire, on an island of Druid priestesses,
you transform yourself into a black dog, a raven,
a will-o'-the-wisp, a dragon?
Speak to me, Heloise. The wind, the sea,
do you lift them with your songs?
Tell me, what has happened to you?
"I know the song
that makes the heavens rend,
that makes the sea startle,
that makes the earth tremble.
All there is to know on earth,
I know it,
I know
all that has been, all that will be.
But I no longer know love.
I say farewell to everyone.
I will never see you again."

From *Elena*

L'isola di Eloisa

Alla foce della Loira, in un'isola di druide,
ti trasformi in cane nero, in corvo
in fuoco fatuo, in drago?
Parlami, Eloisa. Li sollevi
vento e mare con i canti?
Dimmi, che ne è di te?
"Conosco il canto
che fa lacerare i cieli,
trasalire il mare,
tremare la terra.
Quel che c'è da sapere al mondo
io lo conosco,
tutto ciò che è stato, tutto che sarà.
Ma l'amore non lo conosco più,
dico addio a tutti,
io non vi vedrò più."

ESSAYS ON MYTH

ORIGINS
&
TRANSITIONS
TOWARDS A NEW MILLENNIUM

Anna Meda

Myth in the Modern World and the Role of Poetry

I would like to start with a question which is simple enough in its formulation but perhaps not so simple in its possible answers: What is myth?

Today this word "myth" is often used and more often abused especially in everyday language where it is equated to a pure sign, i.e something that stands for something else but—contrary to symbols—has only a univocal meaning. Often it is also exploited for commercial and political purposes. Karl Kerényi distinguished this type of myth from what he called "genuine" myth (Kerényi 153-68), which I shall discuss later.

Definitions of myth abound. They span from the original one of 'sacred' narration of cosmogonic events, of cultural foundation, divine origins and heroic deeds to the allegorical or poetic rendering of an abstract teaching or even the empty shell serving an ideology and aiming at manipulating the masses. In Fascist Italy for instance Mussolini's persona and character were mythologized into larger than life proportions by a carefully constructed propaganda supporting the patriarchal values of virility, war and conquest. The greatness of ancient Rome and the Roman Empire served as a model on which to superimpose the achievements of the Fascist empire. Needless to say the iconography of the period was made up of signs rather than symbols. These signs were empty shells void of any substance like the empty cartridges of the rifles which apparently were sometimes issued to Italian soldiers during World War II. Symbols on the other hand are archetypal images and, as Jung pointed out, " express the unknown, throw a bridge out towards the unseen".[1] They always stand for a meaning beyond our present comprehension.

---

[1] Jung, "On the Relation of Analytical Psychology to Poetry" (76).

The Waters of Hermes/Le acque di Ermes. Edited by Massimo A. Maggiari.

One cannot but feel confused by the variety of definitions, interpretations and usage of the word 'myth'. What is then 'genuine' myth in Kerényi's definition? It is the experience of archaic elements in the psychic life of modern man (Kerényi/Jung 59-60).[2] As such, myth links all acts, thoughts and experiences of our daily life to the sphere of the unknown and to a timeless dimension. Myth is a revelation of the preconscious psyche. It gives an approximate description of an unconscious core of meaning. Without it modern man and woman experience the loss of their psychic past and what Jung called a "rootless consciousness" (Kerényi/Jung 72-77).

In this perspective then myth is a kind of knowledge which goes beyond time and space. It is the most powerful and universal form of narration and explanation of our world. Through symbols and metaphors (which are the privileged carriers of myth) it tells us something about who we are, have been and will be. It is through the images which arise from the depths of the unconscious mind in the form of symbols that truths which transcend wisdom and intelligence come to the surface. These images are similar to those surfacing in dreams, fantasies and artistic creations (Harding 38).

As Anthony Stevens points out, the virtual disappearance of rites of passage from our culture, has disconnected us from our inner, spiritual life, from those deep psychic energies which seek to transform our lives. We are left without a mythic context to give them meaning (Stevens 64). This has brought about a one-sidedness in our culture. Science (our new modern faith) is impotent in face of the threatened breakdown in our culture. Dissatisfaction with many aspects of modern life has brought about a general need of renewal, of a spiritual awakening (Harding 7-8). Modern man and woman, like their ancient predecessors, need to regenerate themselves periodically by re-

---

[2] Kerényi explains the use of the word 'archaic' in this context as follows: "[...] the term 'archaic [has] no chronological significance, though [it has] a strictly scientifical meaning. This meaning lies in the fact that the phenomena so described have an actual correspondance with certain earlier phenomena in the history of mankind, which can be determined chronologically."

actualizing the timeless and universal dimension of myth. As Mircea Eliade once said, " By *living* the myths one emerges from profane, chronically ordered time" and enters a time which is 'different', i.e., sacred and primordial (Eliade, *The Myth of the Eternal Return* 74).

Is it still possible then to do that today? Can we in our modern disenchanted and pre-eminently secular world still '*live the myths*', i.e., enter their sacred dimension?

As we approach the threshold of the new millennium there is a widespread perception of an era coming to an end. A January issue of "Time Magazine", titled "The end of the world", featured articles and reports on the Y2K Syndrome and other apocalyptic doomsdays. The New Age wave and other new spiritual sects and organizations that have mushroomed in the last forty years all seem to point to this need to escape from a narrowly materialistic and venal view in search of new values and meaning.

If in ancient times myths were the foundations of faith and beliefs, today they are the manifestation of the contents of our deeper psyche. As such they appear in our dreams and fantasies and in works of art. It is through art, and poetry in particular, that even today myths still speak to the masses. That's why the coming together of myth and poetry in this festival is particularly significant and meaningful.

The central myth of literature - as Northrop Frye pointed out—is the quest myth, i.e. the heroic quest which takes the shape of a literal or—more often—a metaphorical descent into darkness and peril followed by a renewal of life (Frye 25-26). In the quest the passage from death to revival is in fact a transformation to a new life. The 'new' rituals of modern Western life   (e.g. yoga, meditation, astrology, magic, drugs etc), even though often just a vogue and a fashionable form of escapism, emanate from this subconscious yearning for a renewal of life. This yearning, which is usually confused and unstructured, finds a coherent form in literature, especially in those works which Jung called "visionary" (Jung, "*Psychology and Literature*" 89).

What makes these works so significant is the "vision of deeper things, of primordial images and primitive forces which underlie all life and are its nourishing, sustaining, creative matrix" (Jung, *Symbols of Transformation* 413). It would be much too long and complex to go now into what is art and who is the artist. Let's just say that the special significance of art resides in the fact that it escapes from the limitations of the artist and transcends his/her consciousness. For this reason, rather than being far remote from societal needs, visionary poetry meets the spiritual needs of all human beings, because it acts as mediator between consciousness and the collective unconscious.

It is no coincidence that in so many modern writers there is the need to abolish historical time in order to access a mythical time, i.e. time before and beyond time as we know it. James Joyce and T. S. Eliot are two good examples, and among the many Italian writers we could quote D'Annunzio, Pavese and even Luigi Pirandello, who is better known as the disillusioned bard of the divided self and the perennial tension between reality and illusion, but who also tried to overcome them in his trilogy of myths by seeking for wholeness in the timeless and universal dimension of myth.[3] It is also no coincidence that rebirth and regeneration myths so often appear in the works of these modern writers. In a world where the 'waste land' is not just purely an ecological concern, but rather a condition of our inner landscape plagued by a pervading sense of fragmentation, relativity and loss of our inner life, these myths are ever more relevant.

Since myth has a "more universal and more fundamental language," it compensates our modern "hypertrophy of consciousness" (Jung, *Psychology and Religion* 189-90) by re-actualizing the Great Mother archetype, which is strictly related to all myths of rebirth. In so doing these writers are actually interpreting not only their own needs as individuals but also those of their contemporaries.

Art has a compensatory function to our conscious attitudes. By compensating their one-sidedness it brings back a state of balance. Jung expresses this concept very poignantly: "Whoever speaks in primordial

---

[3] See my own, *Bianche statue contro il nero abisso* for an in-depth analysis of Pirandello's trilogy of myths.

images speaks with a thousand voices; he enthrals and overpowers, while at the same time he lifts the idea he is seeking to express out of the occasional and the transitory into the realm of the ever-enduring. He transmutes our personal destiny into the destiny of mankind. [...] The artist translates [the vision] into the language of the present, and so makes it possible for us to find our way back to the deepest springs of life. Therein lies the social significance of art: it is constantly at work educating the spirit of the age, conjuring up the forms in which the age is most lacking" (Jung, *"On the Relation of Analytical Psychology to Poetry"* 82).

University of South Africa, Pretoria

Anna Meda is Associate Professor in the Department of Romance Languages at the University of South Africa (Pretoria) and a co-editor of Italian Studies in Southern Africa. She has published on Pirandello, D'Annunzio, South African theatre and contemporary writers.

Works Cited

Eliade, Mircea. *The Myth of the Eternal Return*. Princeton: Princeton UP, 1974
_____. "Myths and Mythical Thought." A. Eliot/J.Campbell/M.Eliade. *The Universal Myths*. New York: Meridian, 1990. 14-40.
Frye, Northrop. "The Archetypes of Literature." *Jungian Literary Criticism*. Ed. R. P. Sugg. Evanston: Northwestern UP, 1992. 21-37.
Harding, M. Esther. *Woman's Mysteries. A Psychological Interpretation of the Feminine Principle as Portrayed in Myth, History, and Dreams*. New York: G. P. Putnam's Sons, 1971.
Jung, Carl Gustav. "On the Relation of Analytical Psychology to Poetry." *The Spirit in Man, Art and Literature* 65-83.
_____. "Psychology and Literature." *The Spirit in Man, Art and Literature* 84-105.
_____, *Psychology and Religion*. Vol. 2 of the *Collected Works*. London: Routledge & Kegan Paul, 1970.
_____. *The Spirit in Man, Art and Literature*. Vol. 15 of the *Collected Works*. London: Routledge & Kegan Paul, 1985.
_____, *Symbols of Transformation*. Vol. 5 of the *Collected Works*. London: Routledge & Kegan Paul, 1986.
Jung, Carl Gustav, and Karl Kerényi. *Science of Mythology*. London: Ark, 1985.
Kerényi, Karl. "Dal mito genuino al mito tecnicizzato." *Atti del Colloquio internazionale su* Tecnica e casistica. Roma, 1964.
Meda, Anna. *Bianche statue contro il nero abisso. Il teatro dei miti di D'Annunzio e Pirandello*. Introd. Cesare Segre. Ravenna: Longo, 1993.
Stevens, Anthony. *On Jung*. London: Penguin, 1990.

Larry Simms

Poetry, Myth, and the Shaman

When we consider the origins of poetry and myth, we find a likely progenitor for both in the person of the shaman, whose origins may well go back to the Paleolithic Era (for our purposes, c. 200,000 to c. 10,000 years B.C.). In essence, the shaman functions as an intermediary between his community as a whole, or individual members of that community, and the world of the unknown, the world of divine or demonic powers. Initiation into shamanic practice normally consists of an ordeal, in the form of a serious illness, traumatizing dream, or hallucination often involving the sensation of death and/or dismemberment, followed by rebirth or regeneration. This has been compared to the "traditional schema of an initiation ceremony: suffering, death, resurrection" (Eliade, *Shamanism* 33). Once this ordeal, or at times series of ordeals, has transpired, the newly initiated shaman frequently receives additional training in shamanic lore from a more experienced practitioner, but it is by virtue of the initial death-rebirth experience that he or she is validated as a shaman.

In a state of ecstatic trance, induced by various means, the shaman, or more specifically the soul of the shaman, travels to the underworld or to the heavens to encounter supernatural beings or the souls of ancestors, including those of past shamans. The purpose of this journey may vary, but in general the shaman seeks to acquire knowledge beneficial to his community and often related, especially in prehistoric times, to the very survival of the community. He may also seek to recover the soul of someone suffering from illness or even that of one who has died. The motivation for the shamanic endeavor is social, not personal. He functions as the protector of his group, the mana-laden mediator between that group and the spirit-world, the father-figure who maintains or restores the psychic equilibrium of his community. As

The Waters of Hermes/Le acque di Ermes. Edited by Massimo A. Maggiari.

such he assumes at times the role of group-leader, the apparent precursor of the priest-king, so familiar from a variety of ancient cultures in the Old World and the New.

While in the state of ecstatic trance during which the shaman travels to other worlds, his body often remains inert and lifeless. To all appearances he has died, having undergone separation of body and soul, but this separation is only temporary. Upon the return of his soul from its mediating mission, his body returns to life. As in the initiatory phase of the shaman's vocation, he undergoes a figurative death and rebirth. He returns to life, (the mundane life of ordinary consciousness), transfigured, with powers enhanced, endowed with superior knowledge for the benefit of those on whose behalf he undertook his journey.

Shamanic characteristics have been observed in the deities of various mythic systems, including that of the Greeks. Weston La Barre (*The Ghost Dance: The Origins of Religion* 422) has even suggested the shaman as the prototype of the deity. Likewise, we observe a parallel pattern in the sequence of the hero's adventure: separation from the world of familiar experience, an ordeal leading to some type of initiation (often an encounter with death), and eventual return and reintegration into society with enhanced powers of benefaction. Among Greco-Roman heroes we may cite Herakles, Odysseus and Aeneas, all of whom demonstrate shamanic characteristics in their adventures. However, the most notable figure from Greek myth to exemplify shamanic features (and probable shamanic origins) is Orpheus.

Orpheus is said to be either the son or pupil and devotee of the northern god Apollo with whom more shamanic figures are associated than with any other Greek deity. By his incantatory skills he exercises power over nature in the form of wild animals, trees, stones and the waves of the sea, a power not unlike that of some of the shamans of Siberian legend. He is even able to out-sing the death-dealing Sirens. His descent to the house of Hades to bring back his deceased consort Eurydice appears to have been successful in the earliest version of the tale. Moreover, while in the Underworld he is said to have received instruction in the sacred Mysteries. In some accounts his death takes the form of dismemberment at the hands of Thracian Maenads, but his head continues singing and after burial becomes the site of an oracle. His incantatory powers are memorialized in the *Orphic Hymns*, and a religious movement involving abstinence and purification leading to spiritual ecstasy bears his name. In Greek tradition he became the proto-poet and instructor of other legendary poets such as Musaeus, Linus, and Eumolpus. He provides a clear example of shamanic features surviving in a figure who is considered by some to have possible historical origins.

The role of the poet is particularly relevant to our discussion, inasmuch as shamans themselves may well have created the first poetry of our species. As he prepares to enter the ecstatic state, the shaman often chants in a rhythmic fashion, speaking at times a secret or "animal" language which may represent an attempt to call forth his guardian animal-familiar. Rhythmic drumming not infrequently accompanies this chant or incantation. In this rhythmic drumming and chanting we may detect the beginnings of lyric verse and in the secret language may germinate the seeds of poetic expression. In the opinion of Eliade (*Shamanism* 510) the shaman through his secret language creates "a personal universe"; he re-creates language from his own inner experience and in so doing he "reveals the essence of things."

Moreover, it is characteristic of shamanic practice, especially in Siberia and Australia, that the shaman narrates his adventures after his return from his ecstatic journey. These narratives, often preserved orally over long periods of time, frequently feature a descent to the underworld as well as a struggle with opposing spirits. At times the shaman may even be given a song or incantation by the ancestral spirits. These early narratives of shamanic exploits have been suggested as a kind of proto-mythology, with the shaman serving as the guardian or preserver of his community's mythological lore. Furthermore, the shaman is one who "sees" into things hidden from the sight of normal people; he is endowed with "fire of the eyes"; he visualizes mental images which constitute the fundamental components of myth and legend. The oldest term for "poet" in Latin, *vates*, originally meant "seer," "prophet" or "(divinely) inspired singer," in contrast with the later term *poeta*, "one who fashions or contrives." The cognate verb *vaticinor* includes among its meanings "to sing (or chant) by inspiration," "to celebrate in verse," which describes the manner in which the shaman informs and enlightens his community.

According to Andreas Lommel (*Prehistoric and Primitive Man* 20) the shaman's role as performance artist may, in fact, assume even greater significance than his social function as magician, physician and priest. In Lommel's words: "The entire process of becoming and operating as a shaman is essentially a creative, artistic process. The shaman loses consciousness and gives expression to his creative, subconscious mind. He fashions images in his mind as a communication with the spirits. He visualizes the shifting of his level of consciousness as a journey into the beyond."

Another relevant feature of the shamanic experience, as noted by Lommel (19), is that a man "becomes a shaman not by his own volition, but because he is forced to by a feeling that it is his vocation ... he seems to be under a pressure from which he can escape only by becoming a shaman." The parallel with the often compelling force of poetic inspiration becomes immediately apparent. We may well agree with Lommel, Eliade, and others that shamans represent the originators of poetry, as well as drama and dance. In their rhythmic drumming and chanting may be born the first lyric poetry. In the chanted narratives of their exploits in another world, we may look for the beginnings of heroic epic, and in their ecstatic journeys and initiatory ordeals we may glimpse the earliest manifestations of heroic achievement. The shaman seeker who brings hidden knowledge from the world of the supernatural prefigures the culture-hero. The shaman-intermediary who rescues wandering souls from opposing spirits prefigures the epic warrior-hero. The shaman narrator prefigures the oral poet, the guardian and transmitter of tribal myth and tradition. In the prehistoric shaman we may discover the proto-seer creating proto-mythology in the earliest attempts at human poetic expression.

College of Charleston

Larry Simms is an associate professor of Classics at the College of Charleston. He has taught Comparative Mythology and is interested in Jungian Studies.

José Escobar

Origins and Transitions: Meso-America

A fundamental and the very first duty of the ancient Mexicans and those living in ancient Meso-america was to provide nourishment: *intonan intota tlaltecuhtli tonatiuh*, "four our mother and our father, the earth and the sun." To abandon or forsake this duty was to betray the gods, the universe, life, and at the same time, all humankind, for what was true of the sun was also true of the earth, rain, plants, all beings, growth and all the forces of nature. Nothing, absolutely nothing, in their worldview would or could endure unless a reciprocal relationship was established by the blood of sacrifice.

The ancient *Mexicas*, like many other Meso-American peoples, believed that several successive worlds had existed before the present one and that each of them had fallen victim or come to an end amid cataclysms in which humankind had been wiped out. These were the 'four suns,' and the age in which we live is the fifth. Consequently, their belief system, their mythology, was rooted in a process of new origins and transitions, of beginnings and ends, which were intricately linked to certain cosmic dramas and the structure of the universe itself in which the gods sacrificed themselves, immolated themselves, in order to bring forth the world, life, and all beings.

Two primordial beings who were at the origin of all others, even of the gods — *Ometecuhtli*, "The Lord of Duality," and *Omecihuatl*, "The Lady of Duality" — lived and dwelled in the thirteenth heaven. Out of this pair and their fruitfulness, emerged all the gods and humankind. The gods, descendants of the original pair or duality, were the creators of the world and life, the most important being the birth of the sun which was born from sacrifice and blood. In some accounts from the Central Valley of Mexico, it is said that the gods gathered in the twilight at *Teotihuacan*, and one of them, *Nanahuatzin*, a little leprous, poor god, covered with boils, threw himself into a huge fire as a

The Waters of Hermes/Le acque di Ermes. Edited by Massimo A. Maggiari.

sacrifice. He rose from the blazing coals changed into a sun; but this new sun would not move, the idea being that it needed blood to move. So the gods decided to call on *Ehecatl*, an early manifestation of *Quetzalcoatl* as the "Wind before the Rain," to slay them—all fifteen hundred of them—and the newly created sun, drawing life from their death, began its course across the sky.

Because the world had existed on four previous occasions and because the worlds and existence were seen as continually unstable and in a state of crisis and flux by the interaction of forces and energies that needed to be renewed and nourished, all things, including human beings had to reciprocate by sacrifice what was given and brought into beings by sacrifice. Moreover, in order for the world and life to continue, it was imperative to give back the *chalchihuatl*, "the precious water," as nourishment to the world and life. Thus, sacrifice became a sacred duty—even when carried to extremes by any standards— towards the sun, the world, life and the welfare of all beings. Without it, the very life of the world would stop. Nothing would be born, nothing would endure.

In Meso-American mythology death and life are no more two sides of the same reality. Life comes out of death, as the young plant of maize comes from the moldering seed in the earth. As a matter of fact, one name assigned to the maize plant among the people inhabiting the Central Valley of Mexico is *tonacaya*,"our flesh." There is no distinction made between corn and humans; they are closely linked to each other and the death of one means life for the other and vice-versa. Corn is life, flesh, blood, a relative. The same way that corn gives of itself to feed humans, humans must give of themselves to feed the world. This fundamental tenet of the belief system of the ancient *Mexicas* is intricately connected to the structure of the universe itself as conceived by them and is built on reciprocity. As participants in the drama and struggle of existence, they did not see themselves as necessarily different from any other living thing. We are born and are nourished; we grow old and die. This was the rhythm of life, the very quick of life. In other words, everything that has life dies and nourishes a process of continuity. Life has a limit and so does the world and they are always in a state of crisis; no one knows when they will end. Their hope was that by somehow feeding the world and the sun, life would continue, the sun would rise again and for one more hour, one more day, one more year, fifty-two more years (where the two calendars would coincide), existence would prevail.

One fundamental principle of great relevance to the world view of the peoples of the Central Valley of Mexico is the geometry of the universe itself. This idea of its structure and dynamics was widely spread among all Meso-American cultures and shares similarities with other American traditions. Central to this world view is the dual opposition of contrary elements which divide the universe and which at the same time account for its diversity, its order, and its dynamics. Sky and earth, heat and cold, light and darkness, death and life, man and woman, were or are conceived to be polar and complimentary pairs, their elements somehow interrelated by their opposition. The universe itself was conceived as a horizontal plane that basically separated the Great Father from the Great Mother. More complex structures were added as the ancient *Nahuas* perceived the universe as divided into thirteen celestial and nine underworld levels. Each heavenly and underworld level was populated by gods often depicted as a conjugal pair, for example, *Mictlantecuhtli* and *Mictecacihuatl,* "Lord and Lady of Death," expressing the essential duality of existence. The earth itself was imagined as a rectangle or disc (perhaps even a four-petaled flower) surrounded by water and elevated on its four edges to form a wall that supported the sky. Furthermore, the earth was divided into four segments and each had assigned to it a different color, symbols, cardinal point, and at its center, was the axis, the navel of the world. Four sacred trees (in most accounts cypresses) arose from each edge to hold the sky. These trees had many other functions, but along the axis of the cosmos, its center, of this beautiful flower, ran the paths traversed by the sacred beings and their forces in order to reach the earth and exert their influence. From the four trees, the gods of the upper and lower levels, from each and every direction, acted upon the earth, moving toward the central point, bringing time and destiny, shaping and transforming everything in existence. And at its center lived the old god, mother and father of all things, *Huehueteotl*, lord of fire and the catalyst of transformation and change in the nature of all beings. This old god of fire of very ancient origins eventually will merge in the mind of the *Mexicas* and other *Nahua* peoples into the fifth sun, *Tonatiuh*, who occupied a central position in the sky, but also in the hearth. And like the fire in the hearth, consuming and transforming, it had to be fed. This was a sacred duty, the most frequent act of piety and religiosity performed by priests in public ceremonies as well as the duty of every human beings. This was the *nextlahualiztli* , "the act of payment," the giving of the precious liquid, the giving back to life from which life had been taken. As human beings, they did not see themselves separate from any other being inhabiting the world. They took life and sacrificed other animals and plants to nourish themselves and in order to perpetuate this nourishment, they gave back and offer sacrifice to this life itself. It is reciprocity taken to the extreme, perhaps, but nonetheless an idea deeply imbedded in the psyche of the peoples of Meso-America and by which they express the highest form of expression of their religious practices. Like the sun in the sky and the fire in the hearth, everything was in a constant state of flux and transformation and humans were an integral part of the dynamics of the universe and life, not something separate. Humans were responsible for the well-being of life and the world; they had a role to play in perpetuating life, just as the gods had played a role in the creation of the four previous worlds and the fifth, the present one. Now the human race reaches its culminating form where equilibrium and balance are found between the forces that permeate and act upon the universe.

The concept of creation and destruction as a dual but complimentary pair is consistent with the fundamental beliefs of the people of Meso-America. The *Nahuas* believed that the world had gone through several cycles of creation and destruction. Each of these worlds, eras, or "suns" had different characteristics and was ruled by a particular sacred being. At some point in each era, an imbalance brought about destruction and chaos leading to a cataclysm, and finally to a new creation or origin. The essential concept or idea conveyed by this myth is one mixed with dread and hope. On the one hand, the universe or the world will come to an end but from this end will emerge a new beginning or a new creation. Once again, life will arise from death and set the conditions for a new or another cycle. As it is obvious from readings and accounts on Meso-American mythology, creation always takes place through the play or interaction of opposites. Dualities fight or cooperate with each other in order to bring destruction or a new origin. Each universe or world is a by-product of strife or sacrifice.

According to *Mexica* accounts, we live in the fifth sun, which will be destroyed by cataclysmic earthquakes on "a day 4-movement" according to their ritual calendar. The emergence of the fifth sun took place in *Teotihuacan*, where the gods had met to recreate the sun and to give life to the world. Two gods, *Tecciztecatl*, who was wealthy and handsome, and *Nanahuatzin*, the "Little One covered with boils," competed for the honor to jump in a fire and become the sun. The account continues by telling us that *Tecciztecatl* claimed the right to be the first to jump, but his heart filled with cowardice and he balked. *Nanahuatzin* did not hesitate and immolated himself, thus becoming the sun. *Tecciztecatl*, ashamed, followed him, becoming the moon. Yet, the sun would not move and it was in need of nourishment in order to begin its creative process, so the other gods voluntarily called upon *Ehecatl* to slay them and draw their blood to nourish the sun and enable it to move. Thus, the gods sacrificed themselves to create the world and the animal and plant life; humankind was indebted to them for this act of kindness towards humans and life in general. The self-sacrifice of the gods, however, was not sufficient to guarantee the existence of the world or life; the sun now had to be nourished on a daily basis in order to continue its creative role. Humankind's primary responsibility became the feeding of the sun made possible by warfare and through the sacrifice of blood. Although this responsibility was taken quite literally by many in Meso-America and no doubt became a political tool of intimidation in the hands of rulers and the powerful, the roots of this myth are to be found in the basic idea of the interrelatedness of all life. This is the fundamental message or lesson to be learned from these accounts. Nothing comes without consequences to the other and every action leads to the possible extinction or birth of new life. Everything gives of itself and dies in order to allow something else to live. If we are fully aware of this interaction, we have no choice but to live in gratitude.

Finally, I would like to relate, as a closing statement, the myth of the creation of humankind, which once again embodies the theme of sacrifice. The *Mexicas* and other *Nahuas* believed that *Quetzalcoatl* descended to *Mictlan*, "The Place of Death," to retrieve and gather the bones of the inhabitants of the first sun from the lord of the underworld. After facing many obstacles and difficult tasks imposed by the *Mictlantecuhtli*, "Lord of Death," *Quetzalcoatl* began to return to earth with the bones; according to several accounts, however, he was chased by a quail sent by the "Lord of Death," who wanted to break the deal he had made with *Quetzalcoatl*. *Quetzalcoatl*, after a long journey, dropped the bones which where then pecked and broken by the quail. He wept and gathered the pieces that were left and returned to earth and presented the bones to the gods, who grounded them to a powder. *Quetzalcoatl* then pierced his penis and bled himself, thus fertilizing with his blood the bones of the ancients. After four days, a male child emerged from the clay pot where the pulverized bones where being kept, and a female child followed four days later. All humankind descends from this pair, according to the *Nahua* people. We are the product of the gods' penance, the gods' sacrifice; we are the *macehualtin*, "the one who deserved and were brought back to life out of sacrifice." In a dialogue translated by León Portilla between some *Mexica* priests and Spanish friars, the priests answered the friars' question about origins in this fashion:

> It was the doctrine of the elders
> that there is life because of the gods;
> with their sacrifice, they gave us life.
> In what manner? When? Where?
> When there was still darkness.

College of Charleston

José Escobar is an associate professor of Spanish at the College of Charleston. His area of interest is Spanish Medieval and Golden Age Literatures. He has taught for years a course on Medieval Spanish Mysticism.

Dino S. Cervigni

Dante's Judeo-Christian Mytho-Poiesis

Dante never employs the word myth. Dante scholars, by contrast, often use this term, albeit not in the singular but in the plural. Accordingly, they analyze Dante's exploitation and transformation of classical myths, present primarily in the *Divine Comedy*. Take for instance the recently published acts of a Dante seminar entitled: *Dante: mito e poesia*. In this volume myths are mostly studied individually and/or within the specific context in which Dante situates them. Throughout the whole volume, however, time and again there surfaces the issue as to the relationship of both classical and contemporary myths (such as the myth of Ulysses and Florence, respectively) to the overall story, indeed myth, unfolding not only in the *Divine Comedy* but also in Dante's *oeuvre* in its entirety. By contrast, where the term is employed as a collective singular noun, myth is studied, for instance, in its relationship with symbolism, as in Marthe Dozon's impressive study entitled *Mythe et symbole dans la* Divine comédie. Here the scholar seeks to interpret the Dantean myth on the basis not only of studies of myths and religions but also cultural anthropology and Jungian psychology.

Both critical approaches are highly commendable, no matter how different their results may be, and both also advance the scholar's understanding of myth in Dante. In proposing to study myth in Dante from a different perspective, which nevertheless surfaces repeatedly in both volumes, I intend to take stock of the results of the two different approaches outlined above. Thus, while relying on the research of individual myths conducted by Dante scholarship, I bear in mind the myths' role primarily within the *Divine Comedy*, whose ultimate meaning can be uncovered only through the understanding of medieval culture in its Christian perspective.[1]

---

[1] A very comprehensive treatment of Dantean myths, Dozon's volume includes in her discussion virtually every aspect of the *Divine Comedy* related to myth, allegory, and symbol. The volume *Dante: mito e poesia* is fragmented into hardly related analyses of specific myths in Dante (Dante and myths; the myth

The Waters of Hermes/Le acque di Ermes. Edited by Massimo A. Maggiari.

At the basis of my approach lies a deeply felt personal conviction grounded on decades of familiarity with Dante: a notion shared, I believe, by most contributors to *Dante: mito e poesia*, by Marthe Dozon, and all those scholars who dealt with Dante in the miscellaneous volume just mentioned. Accordingly, Marthe Dozon writes that the "I-narrator" of the *Divine Comedy* presents himself as the hero of a *fabula* that draws its models from classical myths, such as those of Hercules, Orpheus, Theseus, and Aeneas, which are transformed by Dante's poetic genius into the itinerary of a soul engaged in a spiritual quest (33). Moving along similar critical perspectives, in *Dante: mito e poesia* Michelangelo Picone emphasizes Dante's transformation of all classical and contemporary myths into a unifying Christian perspective.[2] I fully share Picone's synthesis of the role of classical myths in Dante and of their total absorption into the Christian myth. At the same time, while pursuing a similar critical perspective, I would like to propose an even more comprehensive approach to Dante's myth.

In is my critical belief, in fact, that the overall content and structure of Dante's *oeuvre*, primarily the *Vita nuova* and *Divine Comedy*, but all

---

of Orpheus; the myth of Circe; etc.). Some essays, however, focus somewhat more directly on the overarching presence of the Christian myth (Güntert; Kleinhenz). In his introduction and conclusion to the volume (21-32; 437-39), Michelangelo Picone suggests the possibility of viewing Dante's *oeuvre* from the all-comprehensive perspective of the Christian myth that I outline in this essay.

[2] In his introduction Picone writes: "Se l'*Inferno* è la cantica che descrive la degradazione del peccatore verso forme di vita animale, vegetale e perfino minerale, il *Purgatorio* è invece la cantica che affabula il processo di recupero da parte del penitente di una forma di vita autenticamente umana. Dalla deformazione e perversione infernale si passa così alla *reformatio* e *conversio* purgatoriale" (27). "Passando dal *Purgatorio* al *Paradiso* la tematica della *reformatio*, del restauro dell'immagine divina dell'uomo, cede il posto alla tematica della *deificatio*" (30). In the volume's conclusion Picone returns to this idea: "Le verità più alte del mistero cristiano—la trinità, l'incarnazione di Cristo—sono chiaramente presentate come i nuovi miti moderni che hanno preso il posto dei vecchi miti della poesia classica. La riscrittura del mito classico può dirsi in questa maniera completata, esaurita. Il poema delle nuove metamorfosi cristiane—la *Commedia*—ha definitivamente sostituito il poema delle vecchie metamorfosi pagane, e Dante ha preso il posto di Ovidio" (438).

the other works as well, rest on the fourfold Judeo-Christian myth that fully encompasses man's existence: humankind's creation, fall, renewal, and redemption. This complex *mythos* is capable of explaining not only the countless Judeo-Christian myths in Dante's *oeuvre* but also all classical, primordial, and contemporary myths.

Within the strictures of this essay, I need only deal summarily with the meaning and function of myth in general, referring first to one of the most famous employers of the term in reference to poetry.[3] In his *Poetics*, of the six elements making up tragedy, Aristotle considers *mythos*, i.e., story or plot, first and foremost. In the Aristotelian notion of drama, *mythos* corresponds to real life's action, which is understood not only as an external act but rather as an inward and rational process, encompassing, therefore, all those elements, both internal and external, working together towards a definite purpose. In brief, in a broader application of what Aristotle says of the term's function in reference to tragedy (*Poet.* vi. 14), *mythos* constitutes the soul of literature.[4]

Understood in this manner, *mythos* goes also beyond another explanation of the term, according to which myth "is a narrative or group of narratives which recount the activities of a culture's gods and heroes" (Vickery 806). In fact, the term's full import may be best understood through Franco Ferrucci's terse claim that no fundamental difference exists between myth and literature. Thus, reversing Northrop Frey's definition of literature as "reconstructed myth," Ferrucci views myth as literature's primordial form, in accordance with some of the greatest contemporary scholars of myth criticism (513).[5]

I have just proposed above that Dante's *oeuvre* is constructed on a fourfold Judeo-Christian myth, which functions as an all-pervasive master story or narrative: humankind's beginning, fall, conversion, and

---

[3] For an excursus on myth in Greek literature, see Zimmermann's essay in *Dante: mito e poesia* (33-40).

[4] I have here summarized S. H. Butcher's analysis of Aristotle's notion of *mythos* (334-67).

[5] I refer the reader to Ferrucci's essay, with extensive bibliographical notes, for a fundamental discussion of the notion of myth, in which he also deals with Dante. In English see pertinent entries (with bibliography) in the *New Princeton Encyclopedia of Poetry and Poetics*. In *Dante: mito e poesia* see especially Güntert's contribution.

glorification. Dante scholars know full well the extent to which such a Judeo-Christian myth pervades Dante's work. At the same time, only reluctantly do they approach Dante's poetic genius from this perspective because of what we can call an allergy to an approach often considered excessively religious. Dante's poetic genius, however, is grounded upon this Judeo-Christian myth, which forms the all-encompassing master narrative of his *oeuvre* and into which all pagan and contemporary myths are being grafted.

To circumvent such a critical allergy to an apparently excessively religious approach, while still doing justice to the Dantean fourfold Judeo-Christian myth, I would like to propose a theoretical approach that is equally founded on myth, is all-comprehensive, and is based primarily, albeit not exclusively, on Northrop Frye's composite approach to literature and myth. To seek to read Dante's *oeuvre* by means of Frye's critical approach should, at first sight, surprise no one. In fact, just as Dante was influenced by the Bible more so than by any other book, Frye's literary analyses over the course of several decades have constantly revolved around the Bible, as he himself acknowledges (*The Great Code* xiv).

At the basis of Frye's critical method lies his claim that the scholar should not be concerned about uncovering poetry's truths or any relationships between literature and reality, but rather about revealing certain patterns that form a poetic universe of their own. Especially in his *Anatomy of Criticism*, Frye develops a fourfold approach: 1) Historical criticism, or theory of modes, including the fictional, the tragic, the comic, and the thematic; 2) Ethical criticism, or theory of symbols, including the literal, descriptive, formal, mythical, and anagogic; 3) Archetypal criticism, or theory of myths, according to the year's four seasons: Spring, Summer, Autumn, and Winter, which correspond to literature's traditional four genres, respectively: comedy, romance, tragedy, and irony and satire; and finally 4) Rhetorical criticism, or theory of genres: epos, prose, drama, and lyric.

It is a truism that Dante's genius escapes easy definitions and synthesizing attempts. Nevertheless, judiciously employed and further enriched by other critical approaches, Frye's fourfold approach provides a comprehensive hermeneutical approach to Dante's poetic rendering of the fourfold Judeo-Christian onto which primordial, classical, and contemporary myth is being grafted and is thus imbued with a totally different meaning.

Relying on principles laid out by Aristotle in his *Poetics*, Northrop Frye's criticism focuses on four narrative categories or generic plots, organized according to two opposite pairs and aimed at explaining literature as a whole: tragedy and irony or satire, on the one side, and comedy and romance, on the opposite side. Furthermore, Frye illustrates his fourfold archetypal myth by means of the four seasons marking the passing of human time: the mythos of spring as comedy, the mythos of autumn as tragedy, the mythos of winter as irony and satire, and the mythos of summer as romance.

These different frames of reference — the Judeo-Christian *mythos* of humankind's creation, fall, renewal, and redemption, which incorporates all myths exploited by Dante, and Frye's fourfold archetypal myth — can be employed side by side to understand and explain Dante's art, which I would like to call mytho-poiesis. Within the proposed critical perspective, Frye's approach provides a composite hermeneutics capable of explaining Dante's employment and transformation of myths, while the Judeo-Christian approach offers the ultimate moral, intellectual, and teleological perspective pervading all religious elements, rituals, and beliefs at the basis of his *oeuvre*.

Let us briefly present Dante's fourfold Judeo-Christian mytho-poiesis.

As in Christianity, Dante the poet's myth of beginning is twofold: man's primordial condition of innocence right after creation and before the fall, and, after the fall, man's restored condition of innocence through Christ's Redemption. Both stages of innocence can be comprised within Frye's mythos of spring and the genre of comedy.

Just as in the Judeo-Christian tradition, Dante's myth of innocent beginning, a comedic phase, is tragically interrupted by the fall of the hero. The myth of the fallen hero, therefore, is that of autumn, which expresses a transitional phase; tragedy is the genre best suited to render the hero's fall caused by his moral wrongdoing.

Although fallen and thus turned almost into a villain, the Dantean hero is nevertheless allowed to resume his interrupted quest. Thus, like such biblical figures as Jonah and Christ and such classical heroes as Orpheus, Hercules, and Aeneas, he must undertake a journey through the underworld, the realm of darkness, sterility, and eternal suffering. As the perversion of what creation was intended to be and thus the parody of the spring-like myth of beginnings before the fall or Eden, the Christian underworld is best expressed through the myth of winter and the genre of satire.

After descending to the underworld as a *conditio sine qua non* for him to continue his quest, the hero resurfaces on the shores of Mount Purgatory, aware of having lost his way in the past and of finally resuming the right journey. Thus the purgatorial journey constitutes a new beginning after the fall. Once again, Dante the poet ushers in a story that begins somberly but leads to a happy ending. In archetypal criticism, the hero's ascent through the seven terraces of Mount Purgatory corresponds to that season in the year when nature leaves behind the lifeless winter and gradually, through early spring, readies to its rebirth. In this narrative, early spring is best expressed by the genre of comedy. At the top of Mount Purgatory the Dantean hero enters the Earthly Paradise, where he experiences spiritual rebirth and inner transformation, best expressed through the myth of full spring and the genre of comedy.

Finally, the hero's ascent to heaven, in the company of Beatrice, cannot but belong to the myth of summer, with its brightest light and fullness of life. Properly adapted to Dante *oeuvre*, comedy expresses such a state of idealized experience, in which the hero ascends, and is in fact likened, to the gods.[6]

The University of North Carolina at Chapel Hill

Dino S. Cervigni teaches Italian literature at the University of North Carolina at Chapel Hill and has published on the Renaissance and Middle Ages, especially on Dante.

Works Cited

Alighieri, Dante. *La commedia secondo l'antica vulgata.* Ed. Giorgio Petrocchi. 4 vols. Milano: Mondadori, 1966-67.

_____. *Vita nuova. Italian Text with Facing English Translation.* Trans. and

---

[6] In a forthcoming essay I will further develop the nucleus of ideas presented in this brief essay.

ed. Dino S. Cervigni and Edward Vasta. Notre Dame: The U of Notre Dame P, 1995.

_____. *Opere minori* Tome 1, part 1. Ed. Domenico De Robertis and Gianfranco Contini. *Vita nuova.* Ed. Domenico De Robertis. *Rime.* Ed. Gianfranco Contini. *Il fiore* e *Il detto d'amore.* Ed. Gianfranco Contini. Milano: Ricciardi, 1984.

_____. *Opere minori.* Tome 1, part 2. *Convivio.* Ed. Cesare Vasoli and Domenico De Robertis. Milano: Ricciardi, 1988.

_____. *Opere minori.* Tome 2. *De vulgari Eloquentia.* Ed. Pier Vincenzo Mengaldo. *Monarchia.* Ed. Bruno Nanrdi. *Epistole.* Ed. Arsenio Frugoni and Giorgio Brugnoli. *Egloge.* Ed. Enzo Cecchini. *Questio de Aqua et Terra.* Ed. Francesco Mazzoni. Milano: Ricciardi, 1979.

Butcher, S. H. *Aristotle's Theory of Poetry and Fine Art with a Critical Text and Translation of the* Poetics. Pref. John Gassner. New York: Dover, 1951.

Dante: mito e poesia. Atti del secondo Seminario dantesco internazionale (Monte Verità, Ascona, 23-27 giugno 1997). Ed. Michelangelo Picone and Tatiana Crivelli. Firenze: Franco Cesati Editore, 1999.

Dozon, Marthe. *Mythe et symbole dans la* Divine comédie. Biblioteca dell'Archivum Romanicum, ser. 1, vol. 233. Firenze: Olschki, 1991.

Ferrucci, Franco. "Il mito." *Letteratura italiana. Le questioni* 513-49.

Frye, Northrop. *Anatomy of Criticism: Four Essays.* 1957. New York: Atheneum, 1969.

_____. *Fables of Identity. Studies in Poetic Mythology.* New York: Harcourt, Brace & World, 1963.

_____. *The Great Code. The Bible and Literature.* New York: Harcourt Brace Jovanovich, 1982.

_____. *Words with Power. Being a Second Study of "The Bible and Literature."* New York: Harcourt Brace Jovanovich, 1990.

Güntert, Georges. "Dante autobiografico: dal mito religioso al mito poetico." *Dante: mito e poesia* 117-26.

Kleinhenz, Christopher. "Mito e verità biblica in Dante." *Dante: mito e poesia* 391-404.

Letteratura italiana. Vol. 5. *Le questioni.* Ed. Alberto Asor Rosa. Torino: Einaudi, 1986.

The New Princeton Encyclopedia of Poetry and Poetics. Ed. Alex Preminger and T. V. F. Brogan. Princeton: Princeton UP, 1993.

Vickery, John B. "Myth." *The New Princeton Encyclopedia of Poetry and Poetics.*

_____. "Myth Criticism." *The New Princeton Encyclopedia of Poetry and Poetics.*

Zimmermann, Bernhard. "Funzioni del mito nella letteratura greca." *Dante: mito e poesia* 42-48.

William Willeford

Hermes: Poetic Truth, Lying, and Thievery

We read poetry partly because we know it to effect a transformation of the world or of our understanding of it, and because we earnestly if not always consciously desire this.

Such poetic transformation we think of as an elevation — of what the poet is talking about, and hence of the reader. Or — to reverse the image, we think of poetry as bringing something superior down to us. Either way, we may associate poetry with divinity, which often resides in such heights as the sky and mountaintops, and may imagine it as the source of poetry.

Poetry also calls up thoughts of divinity in making us feel that we now, having read something poetic, understand more truly what we need to understand than we did before. And we may imagine that what is truer is higher, as divinity often is.

But already we might pause to think: The eternal gods, however knowing and transparent to truth, must also live in time, since the sky and mountaintops have weather, which is temporal indeed, and so are subject to change and contingency.

When we call poetry "hermetic" after the god Hermes, we mean that it expresses the inmost essence of something in an arcane way, circumventing or baffling conventional reasoning. Only some kinds of poetry are hermetically obscure, of course. But there is something obscure in the background of poetry more generally. This obscure thing is known by such names as life, which is there to be taken into account in something of its obscurity. Also, more generally, Hermes as a god of poetry may be thought to embody a creative principle that dissolves or darkens to the end of bringing something new and valuable to light.

It may not, however, be granted us readers to see the new thing. Instead we may see the darkening that precedes its emergence — if

The Waters of Hermes/Le acque di Ermes. Edited by Massimo A. Maggiari.

indeed it is truly there, its existence till it emerges being a matter of faith or hope.

Hermes lives much of the time with the other high gods on Olympus, a place of relative permanence. Still, he is "mercurial" — his Roman name is Mercury — and so he has a special affinity with the change, contingency and dissolution that are ceaselessly present in poetic transformation (as in Olympian weather). He is their agent. Perhaps it is even true that nothing poetic can be securely possessed, any more than anything is safe in the company of thieves. Hermes, after all, was a thief almost from his birth.

I mention his thievery almost as an aside, and this is fitting, because thieves often sidle up to their victims. But thievery and the making of art are in any case in some ways related. It is reported that when Picasso visited Matisse in his studio, Matisse knew that Picasso was going to rob him with his eyes by looking around at his most recent work.

Since Hermes is so famously and charmingly friendly, however, it might be friendlier to him to downplay his thievery. We might say instead that, yes, poetic transformation entails a certain dissolution of what was there before but that this is just a softening of boundaries that prepares the way for something new to be visible. Still, such a relativization brings about a diminution of some elements and in this sense a loss. And for that matter, a friendly thief like Hermes may rob you even more effectively than an unfriendly one.

As I consider how Hermes relativizes things and to what effect, I wonder how truthful poetic expression truly is. And so I wonder how truthful the gods really are who are thought to inspire it. That Hermes may lie we know from many stories, but does his power to do so relativize into falsehood the poetic truth that now concerns me? He is, after all, only one of the gods; lying is only one of the things he does, and it offers one way of imagining poetic transformation.

Let us for a moment consider an instance of poetic transformation remote from any reference to the gods: the phrase "adagio of islands" from *Voyages* (II) by the twentieth-century American poet Hart Crane. This phrase seems to present us with something radically new and original, a vision of fixed and stable islands brought into slow, dance-like movement, perhaps transposed from crude matter to whatever space musical sound might be thought to inhabit, as random outcroppings from the water are made to reveal a measured, beautiful order. We might think, by the way, that it is their immersion in water, the element of dissolution, that allows them thus to be transformed.

Yet even quite non-poetically, we know that islands are not really solid at all. Rather, lacking firm edges, they are caught up in a gradual but ceaseless process of transformation. The workaday parts of our minds accommodate islands to the reality of maps, real estate, profit and loss, and industry and commerce, and so make us forget their fluidity and vitality. Such a phrase as "adagio of islands" make us remember such qualities suppressed in our knowledge of islands as ordinary things. But then again, what the phrase makes us see anew we have in another sense known all along.

One way of picturing the relation of poets to divinity and whatever higher view of things they may have is offered by the Muses, who reveal things as though anew but who are the daughters of Mnemosyne, or Memory. It is thus by getting us to remember what we already know that they help the poet to express something of the wisdom of their divine father Zeus.

One of the great Western philosophers of memory is, of course, Plato, whose ideal forms are discovered by a process of remembering. But as is also well known, Plato wanted to banish poets from his Republic. And this judgment brings us to another view of poetry and poets according to which poetry in the final analysis consists of lies and poets are liars. Though seemingly puritanical and curmudgeonly, this sceptical view also has merit and has figured in attempts to imagine the relation of poetry to divinity, including some by Shakespeare.

Since Shakespeare was a master of seeing things in many possible ways, it is not surprising that he also explored the ambiguity that poetry is partly true and partly a lie and it may even be both things at the same time. One place where he does this is in a scene from *A Winter's Tale* (IV, iv), in which young country people, along with a royal prince and princess destined to marry one another — the prince is disguised as a shepherd — are all drawn together at a sheep-shearing feast. There they eat, drink, dance and buy ballads from a rogue, who also sells trinkets that young lovers want to give one another as presents. This trickster and charlatan, the grand architect of the whole occasion, could be regarded as the prototype of the artist, giving people entertainment but also playing upon — and in measure genuinely fulfilling — their deepest longings for something other than their everyday lives. He is also making money from them, even by cheating them and outright picking pockets. The name of this rogue is Autolycus, which is odd in being Greek, since this part of the play is set in Bohemia, but then tricksters are often outsiders. According to one account, Autolycus was the father of the hero Odysseus's mother, and was himself the son of the god Hermes, who gave him the power of stealing whatever he wanted without being caught.

As our thoughts about "adagio of islands" should have suggested, the notion that poetry consists of lies may sometime prove too simple, because it may assume that what we call reality is more straightforward, everyday and matter-of-fact than it ultimately is. After all, islands *are* alive and in movement. Still, truth-telling cannot leave lying behind altogether. It is true in a general way about our subjective lives that whatever is most essential — the thing that contains the seed of wisdom or what matters most for the well-being of our souls — can sometimes only be known by indirection, by being glimpsed in a momentary halflight. And this halflight also harbors rogues, liars and thieves. So if Shakespeare is presenting the trickster Autolycus as the prototype of the artist, this portrayal is not entirely ironic and mocking. After all, the action of the play requires that the disguised prince, the future King, not simply be given his bride but must try to steal her.

Looking more closely at the father of Autolycus, Hermes, it is good to have in mind the qualities we most readily associate with his half-brother Apollo, also a god of poetry, indeed usually the paramount god of that art. These qualities include order, clarity, proportion and harmony, all of which we may hope that poetry will give us. But as our reflections have already shown, much of the poetic value, including the phrase "adagio with islands," comes into being precisely when such qualities are relaxed, compromised or dissolved. Again, it is when Shakespeare's disguised prince becomes a rogue that he demonstrates the rightness of his claim to his bride and his future throne. In any case, the destinies of the two gods are linked from the beginning — at least from the infancy of the younger of them, Hermes. And keeping each of them in mind helps us to have a fuller understanding of the other.

According to *The Homeric Hymn to Hermes*, the god was born "wily boy, flattering and cunning, a robber and cattle thief, a bringer of dreams, awake all night, waiting by the gates of the city" (trans. Lewis Hyde). And his first two deeds, immediately after his birth, were his invention of the lyre, which became the emblem of the poetic art, and his theft of Apollo's cattle.

Hermes made his lyre from a tortoise, which he had to kill and the shell of which he had to scrape clean of its flesh. (*The Homeric Hymn* tells us nothing about this grisly business.) Remarkably, the detailed plan for the lyre somehow appeared fully articulated to him. The complex but hunch-like idea of the lyre could in German be called an *Einfall*, a falling in from above, reminding us of what I have said about heights and divinity. In a more modern parlance, we might describe the plan for the lyre as a product of the unconscious. And indeed we know related psychic products, such as dreams. But our ways of talking again cross one another: If divinity is above, the unconscious most commonly seems below, and if we associate the lyre with light and harmony, we most commonly associate the unconscious with darkness and relative chaos. But this leads me precisely to the point I wish to make: The distinction between high and low and light and dark is relative, and paradoxically, sometimes the only source of light is what is now darkness. Thus if the plan for the lyre were a dream, we would have to immerse ourselves in the darkness of sleep to have access to it. We should also note with regard to the lyre that the tortoise is an ancient, even primordial creature. This should remind us that Mnemosyne, the Memory of often archaic things, is the mother of the Muses, who often create novelty in a way that results in bringing them anew to our awareness.

After creating the lyre, Hermes stole Apollo's cattle and so instigates a quarrel that required the intervention of their father Zeus. In settling it, Hermes gave the lyre to Apollo. And in exchange Hermes was given the functions he carries out as a divinity, including being the sole passenger to the underworld. And so Hermes' link with the shadowy and irrational and with what is below, was made official.

As we have seen, Apollo's lyre, one of the great symbols of the poetic art and its ability to create elevated and harmonious speech, was bequeathed to him by a wily liar and a thief. But we may still ask: Do islands truly move in accord with a time that can be marked adagio? To find this question meaningful we would have — imaginatively — to have seen islands move. And to do this we would need to have passed through a halflight conducive to Hermes and other liars and thieves, known to such poets as Hart Crane and Shakespeare. In this roundabout way we can affirm that there is truly an adagio of islands.

Atlanta, Georgia

William Willeford is a Jungian analyst in practice in Atlanta, Georgia. He taught English and Comparative Literature at the University of Washington, in Seattle, for several years. He is the author of *The Fool and His Scepter. A Study in Clowns and Jesters and Their Audience* (1969) and *Feeling, Imagination and the Self. Transformations of the Mother-Infant Relationship* (1987).

Donald Phillip Verene

Vico's Poetic Wisdom: *La sapienza poetica*

Two of the greatest dialogues of Plato are the *Republic* and the *Symposium*. The latter concerns *eros;* the former concerns the state, including the relation of *poiesis* and the poets to the state. Early in the *Republic,* in relation to his conception of education, Plato restricts poets and the reciters of poems, the *rhapsodes,* to productions that embody the moral ideals of the state. Plato says that, should someone arrive at the city who was inclined to portray any possible subject in poetry, he would be sent with all due honors on to another city, for it is unlawful in Plato's city to represent what is not virtuous. At the end of the *Republic* Plato again takes up the subject of poetry, this time in terms of the question of the relation of philosophy and poetry. He says there is an ancient quarrel over which can properly present the truth. The poet for Plato is a maker of images through powers of imitation, *mimesis.*

In *Die Geburt der Tragödie,* Nietzsche says: "Plato gave posterity the model for a new art form—the novel. This might be described as 'an infinitely enhanced Aesopian fable,' in which poetry is subordinated to dialectical philosophy just as philosophy had for centuries been subordinated to theology—as an *ancilla*" (sec. 14). Nietzsche thus captures the agenda of Western philosophy. In the quarrel, philosophy emerges as the master of truth. This agenda of philosophy as the one master of truth is inherited by Descartes, who founded modern philosophy by a reaffirmation of the quarrel in the *Discours de la méthode.* Descartes identifies philosophy with the scientific spirit and locates this spirit in the concept of method. Truth is produced by his four-step method of right reasoning, and truth is identified with *clarté.* The Cartesian ego is the heart of the theoretical man. To accomplish this, Descartes excludes from truth all that embodies the *ars topica*—poetry, rhethoric and history. These are the

The Waters of Hermes/Le acque di Ermes. Edited by Massimo A. Maggiari.

forms of thought that embody metaphor and memory. They are without method.

In the *Poetics*, Aristotle says: "But the greatest thing by far is to be a master of metaphor. It is the one thing that cannot be learnt from others; and it also is a sign of genius, since a good metaphor implies an intuitive perception of the similarity in dissimilars" (1459a). Genius accomplishes its ends through verisimilitude; it sees connections in the world. The making of metaphor cannot be learned; there is no method for the production of metaphor. Genius arrives at its truths by an art lost in the human soul, the mastery of metaphor. Descartes' method replaces the *ars topica* with the *ars critica*. Method establishes a critical standard whereby truth is separated from error. Only the *ars topica* can provide the *archai* from which to think. It is a scandal to logic, to method, that it cannot provide its own starting points. Descartes, like Prometheus, gives us a means but gives us no guide for its use. Descartes, the inheritor of Prometheus' gift, seated by the fire in a *poêle* in his room in Ulm, passes on his gift of method to mankind. He is the new Prometheus.

Vico, in *La scienza nuova* (1730; 1744) realized that the single problem to be solved by philosophy is its quarrel with the poets. It is in fact a quarrel with myth, as the poets are the recallers of myth, once the age of myth is past and the philosophers have arrived in history. The quarrel with poetry, Vico sees, requires the recovery, by philosophy, of its own origin. Philosophy arrives in Western consciousness through a transformation of mythic relationships into logical and metaphysical ones. Unless philosophy can account for its own origin, it is an orphan in the world, without knowledge or memory of its parents, who are, to use Nietzsche's terms, myth and music.

Vico resolves the ancient quarrel by his conception of poetic wisdom (*la sapienza poetica*). *Philosophia*, the love (*philia*) of wisdom produced by reason, derives from an earlier wisdom that exists in poetic characters, in what Vico calls *universali fantastici*. Vico sees this truth: myths are a form of thought, a first form of wisdom that is accomplished, not by reason, but by *fantasia*. *Fantasia* is the primordial faculty. At the beginning, all men, like all children, are poets; they form the world through the powers of their *fantasia*, and only later does the love of wisdom as reason, with its *universali intelligibili*, emerge. The poets who come after the age of myths are our memory of this primordial power of *fantasia*. They demonstrate the reality of this first power. Philosophy itself must always go back to *fantasia* not only to discover its own origin but also to obtain the metaphors it requires for the starting point of any one of its chains of reasoning.

In an early fragment, Hegel says that Memory (Mnemosyne) is the "absolute Muse." In another early writing (1796) he calls poetry "the teacher of humanity" (*die Lehrerin der Menschheit*). He suggests that philosophers should go to school with the poets to prevent them from becoming "literal-minded," and he calls for the making of a "mythology of reason" (*Mythologie der Vernunft*). The poets are the preservers of memory; it is they who provide the beginning points for the philosopher's pursuit of reason and the whole of experience. This is the Hegel no one knows, who begins his philosophy in these views of the importance of the myth and poetry. One might think that Hegel must have taken such views from Vico, but he did not. Hegel never read Vico. And yet, the Italian Hegelian Benedetto Croce so hoped that there could be a connection between Hegel and Vico that he wrote a fictitious conversation, "An Unknown Page from the Last Months of Hegel's Life," in which an Italian scholar introduces Vico's work to Hegel who, on reading it, reports that Vico's thought is very close to his own.

The historian Paul Hazard said, in *La pensée européenne au XVIII siècle de Montesquieu à Lessing*: "If only Italy had listened to Giambattista Vico, and if, as at the time of the Renaissance, she had served as guide to Europe, would not our intellectual destiny have been different? Our eighteenth-century ancestors would not have believed that all that was clear was true; but on the contrary that 'clarity is the vice of human reason rather than its virtue,' because a clear idea is a finished idea. They would not have believed that reason was our first faculty, but on the contrary that imagination was" (43). The poet saves us from intelligibility, the rational madness that the understanding can induce when it does not go to school with the *fantasia* of the poets.

Fantasia organizes the passions of the soul and makes *eros* possible. There is no method to obtain genius; either it inhabits the soul or it does not. In the *Symposium*, Socrates says that his instructress in the art of *eros* was a woman of Mantinea called Diotima. On one of the occasions on which she spoke to him, Socrates relates, she asked him what he thought to be the cause of *eros*. She then said: "The object of *eros*, Socrates, is not, as you think, beauty." "What is it then?" "Its object is to procreate and bring forth in beauty" (206 E). *Eros* is the urge to procreate both in the body and in the soul. Among those who can create both with soul and with the body are the poets and all who are deserving of the name inventor (209A). *Eros* can be activated in poetry.

Oscar Wilde said: "All bad poetry is sincere"; in like fashion, we can say: "All good poetry is erotic." To go to school with the poets is to obtain education in both *fantasia* and *eros*. Both take the self out of itself. *Fantasia* makes the metaphor. As Vico says, every metaphor is a fable in brief. The fable affects feeling, and when it does it produces motion in the soul. The soul becomes erotic because its movement is not self-contained; instead the soul is taken out of itself, toward the truth of the fable. There is no *fantasia* without *eros*, and the reverse. *Fantasia* stabilizes feeling in the image, but *eros* pulls the soul toward the image. The image presents a truth that appears only in the fable and not in the methodological truths found by the critical understanding.

The little truths are those available to method; the great truths are those reached by *eros*. In the end, the philosopher who includes the love of poetic wisdom within the love of wisdom shares *eros* with the poet. For a long time now philosophy has attempted to live as an orphan, without myth or music. The old quarrel has become ever older. Yet it is never too late to undertake an education. Philosophy might once more become fantastic and erotic.

Emory University

Donald Phillip Verene is Charles Howard Candler Professor of Metaphysics and Moral Philosophy at Emory University. Among his many works, he is the author of Vico's Science of Imagination *(1981),* Hegel's Recollection *(1985),* The New Art of Autobiography *(1991), and* Philosophy and the Return to Self-Knowledge *(1997).*

Festival Closing

Jorge Marbán

Closing Remarks

We are now bringing to end one of the most memorable events that have taken place within the venerable halls of the College of Chalrleston. A warm thanks should be extended to the participants who came from three continents and to the benefactors who made this festival possible. We are grateful also to the assistants and organizers as well as to the readers who generously gave their time to make this event successful.

Two days ago we heard the welcoming remarks by Frank Morris, Chairman of the multipartite Department where Italian is lodged, and of Dr. Conrad Festa, our Provost. We will always remember his sensitive poem where he showed his pride in his Italian heritage and, especially, in the author of *Il Saggiatore*.

That day we heard the distinguished Italian poet Giuseppe Conte give us a definition of the concept of *Mitomodernismo:* "the attempt to rediscover ancient gods in nature, in our soul and in everyday life" and "the power to reinvent, to recreate, to transform, to overcome that materialism which permeates our times in order to allow us to dream of the future." Our first poet was, appropriately, Giuseppe Conte. His poetry, achieving that simplicity full of depth and musicality which only a chosen few can create, left us with a feeling of beauty that will linger. We heard on Thursday the intense poetry of Gabriella Galzio, contemplating with awe the beauty of Sicily, exploring the relationships between Myth and the Archaic and the generation of the world through tears. It is in fact through pain, she reminds us, that life is created. We also heard one of the three Invocations rendered masterfully, in ancient Greek, by professor Larry Simms: first, to the nine Muses; then, on Friday, to Hermes, and today to Artemis.

On Friday we heard the poetry of Roberto Mussapi, in which the concrete is shown to have roots that reach the most hidden and meaningful feelings. We also listened to the delicate poetry of Simone Guers, who discovered the beauty of life in some enchanting and fleeting moments. On Friday, the Round Table on *Origins and Transitions. Towards a New Millennium* brought together a diverse and impressive group of scholars. Anna Meda, armed with her admirable Jungian background, gave us an effective ideological dissection of the myth. José Escobar shared with us his knowledge of the magical and mythical world of the Nahuas of Central Mexico. Larry Simms offered us his skillful development and application of the concept of the shaman. Dino Cervigni introduced us to the notion of myth in Dante's *oeuvre*. William Willeford communicated his ample knowledge of ancient culture and deep psychological insight about the origin of myth; and Donald Verene, with his easy grasp of ideas and explanation of difficult concepts, provided us with some challenging thoughts on Vico.

We began our day today by listening to the enchanting Indian music of Guy Beck from Krisha's Spring Festival. We heard the philosophical reflections in the poetry of Roberto Carifi, speaking to his interior angels with that sadness that reminds us of Giacomo Leopardi. Then we enjoyed the more playful tone of Laura Stortoni, a magician with words, who creates her own poetical space, alongside Penelope, in her inward travelling. We were touched by the deep sincerity and the love of freedom in the poetry of Tomaso Kemeny. We saw the shadows and heard the fragmented voices of Mario Baudino, reconstructed with the seal of an anxious communicator. Finally, we were introduced to Amundsen, the *signore dell'invisibile fiordo*, by Massimo Maggiari's poems, which brought us imposing geographical scenery together with a strong emotional echo.

Myth has been explored and affirmed during these three remarkable days: as deep psychological insights revealing the roots of the collective unconscious, as a source of imaginative wanderings and historical explorations, and as the representative of the power of the spirit over the material world. We have all become richer and wiser and more sensitive to the marvels and complexities of this world.

The College of Charleston

FARE ANIMA

Semestrale di

Poesia

Narrativa

Poetica

Critica letteraria

Traduzione

Cultura

Direzione e redazione:
Gabriella Galzio, Marco Marangoni, Giampiero Marano

Direttore responsabile:
Rosaria D'Amico

Un numero: L. 15.000

Abbonamento annuo (2 numeri):
Italia L. 30.000
Estero L. 40.000
Abbonamento sostenitore: L. 100.000

Versamento tramite vaglia a:
Fare anima, presso *Studio d'Autore*, C.so di Porta
Ticinese, 75
I - 20123 Milano, Italy